CORPORATE GOVERNANCE, FIRM PROFITABILITY, AND SHARE VALUATION IN THE PHILIPPINES

JUNE 2019

ICD
Institute of Corporate Directors

ADB

CONTENTS

TABLES AND FIGURES

Tables

Figures

ABBREVIATIONS

ACGS	ASEAN Corporate Governance Scorecard
ACMF	ASEAN Capital Markets Forum
ADB	Asian Development Bank
AGM	Annual General Meeting
ASEAN	Association of Southeast Asian Nations
ASX	Australian Securities Exchange
CEO	chief executive officer
CGI	Corporate Governance India
CLSA	Credit Lyonnais Securities Asia
ICD	Institute of Corporate Directors
ICGN	International Corporate Governance Network
IIRC	International Integrated Reporting Council
OECD	Organisation for Economic Co-operation and Development
PCSE	panel-corrected standard errors
PLC	publicly listed company
ROA	return on assets
ROE	return on equity
RPT	related party transactions
SEBI	Securities and Exchange Board of India
SEC	Securities and Exchange Commission
SPE	special purpose enterprises
SPV	special purpose vehicles

ACKNOWLEDGMENTS

We would like to acknowledge the support and assistance provided by the following in the preparation of the study:

Asian Development Bank (ADB)

1. Mohd Sani Mohd Ismail, Senior Financial Sector Specialist, Public Management, Financial Sector, and Trade Division, Southeast Asia Department (SERD)
2. Florissa Villaluna Barot, Public Management, Financial Sector, and Trade Division, SERD

Institute of Corporate Directors (ICD) Philippines

1. Jesus Estanislao, Chairman Emeritus
2. Alfredo Pascual, Chief Executive Officer (CEO)
3. Ricardo Nicanor Jacinto, former CEO
4. Roberto Bascon, Jr., Director for Corporate Governance Analytics
5. Cathyrine Perez, Corporate Governance Analyst
6. Regine Marie Cinco, Director for Research and Development
7. Eric Rosales, Former Business Researcher
8. Lara Gianina Reyes, Business Researcher

University of Asia and the Pacific (UA&P)

1. Anna Maria Mendoza, Dean and Associate Professor, School of Management
2. Jodie Claire Ngo, Secretary of the Operations Committee and Faculty Member, School of Management
3. Elsie Laguador, Administrative Officer, School of Management
4. Nicole Valle, Researcher

EXECUTIVE SUMMARY

This study focused on determining the relationship between corporate governance score and each of the following: (i) market capitalization of the firm, (ii) market valuation as measured by Tobin's Q ratio, and (iii) profitability as measured by return on equity. The selection of 73 publicly listed companies in the Philippines was based on having a corporate governance score of 60 and above. Data for 2014–2016 were taken from the audited financial statements of the companies, the database of the Philippine Stock Exchange, and the ASEAN Corporate Governance Scorecard.

The results of the study showed that there is a positive and statistically significant relationship between (i) corporate governance and market capitalization, (ii) corporate governance and market valuation as measured by Tobin's Q ratio, and (iii) corporate governance and profitability as measured by return on equity.

It can be stated that an increase in the corporate governance score of a publicly listed company in the Philippines would mean an increase in its (i) market capitalization, (ii) market valuation as measured by Tobin's Q ratio, and (iii) profitability as measured by return on equity. The results indicate that publicly listed companies which have given importance to the practice of good corporate governance would benefit from this in terms of good financial performance.

1. INTRODUCTION

1.1 ASEAN Corporate Governance Scorecard

The ASEAN Corporate Governance Scorecard (ACGS) is a benchmarking tool based on international best practices for assessing the corporate governance performance of publicly listed companies in the six participating member countries of the Association of Southeast Asian Nations (ASEAN). Launched in 2011, it was an initiative of the ASEAN Capital Markets Forum (ACMF), composed of capital market regulators from the ASEAN member countries, in collaboration with the Asian Development Bank.

The objectives of ACGS are to raise the corporate governance standards of ASEAN publicly listed companies (PLCs), encourage long-term sustainability and resilience of firms, complement the other ACMF initiatives, and promote ASEAN as an asset class to foreign investors. Prior to the design of the ACGS, all six participating countries (Indonesia, Malaysia, the Philippines, Singapore, Thailand, and Viet Nam) already had their national scorecards. Although these scorecards were generally based on international standards, there were obvious differences in assessment methodology, focus areas, and questions. This meant that results of these scorecards were not comparable. In short, there were national champions, but no regional ASEAN champions.

The design of the ACGS is based on the following principles:

(i) reflect global principles and internationally recognized good practices in corporate governance applicable to PLCs;

(ii) encourage PLCs to adopt higher standards and aspirations;

(iii) be comprehensive in coverage;

(iv) identify governance gaps, but also feature good governance practices;

(v) be applicable to different markets in ASEAN;

(vi) provide accurate assessments beyond minimum compliance; and

(vii) provide robust quality assurance to ensure independent and reliable assessment.

The countries participating in the ACGS are Indonesia, Malaysia, the Philippines, Singapore, Thailand, and Viet Nam.

The ACGS covers the five main corporate governance principles promoted by the Organisation for Economic Co-operation and Development:

(i)   rights of shareholders,

(ii)   equitable treatment of shareholders,

(iii)   role of stakeholders,

(iv)   disclosure and transparency, and

(v)   responsibilities of the board.

The ACGS was introduced in the Philippines in 2013 under the auspices of the Securities and Exchange Commission (SEC).[1] Corporate governance assessment based on the ACGS has since been conducted annually by the Institute of Corporate Directors (ICD), the SEC-appointed domestic ranking body in the Philippines.

1.2   ASEAN Corporate Governance Scorecard Performance

From 2012 to 2016, the Philippines steadily improved its corporate governance standing under the ASEAN Corporate Governance Scorecard (ACGS) (Figure 1). Philippine PLCs as a group recorded a low total score of 48.9 during the first ACGS assessment in 2012. This was partially due to the fact that Philippine PLCs were not aware of the requirements of the ACGS, hence the decision of the SEC to join ACGS on a pilot basis. This prompted greater engagements by the SEC and the ICD with the PLCs to explain the requirements of the ACGS and the differences with the national scorecard of the Philippines as well as promote stronger commitment in adopting and implementing the governance practices embedded in the ACGS. Over the following years, a steady improvement was achieved in the total score as well as in the scores in all the five areas of assessment under the ACGS. By 2016, the total score averaged 74.6.

However, the performance for the different areas of assessment was uneven. PLCs in the Philippines generally perform well in the Rights of Shareholders (Part A) and Disclosure and Transparency (Part D) sections. The results in the Part A for 2015 shows that the average score of Philippine PLCs (7.62) was only behind Thailand (9.06), and better than Singapore (7.37) and Malaysia (6.20).[2] Some leading practices include disclosure of voting and vote tabulation procedures in companies' information statements, and minutes of annual shareholders meetings indicate that resolutions adopted during the meetings and are made publicly available the next working day. Although Philippine PLCs also perform well in Equitable Treatment of Shareholders (Part B), the average score of 11.74 in 2015 is still relatively lower than Thailand (14.75), Malaysia (13.04), and Singapore (12.73).

---

[1]   Participation by the Philippines in the first year was on a pilot basis.
[2]   ASEAN Capital Markets Forum and Asian Development Bank. 2016. ASEAN Corporate Governance Scorecard Country Reports and Assessments 2015. Manila.

Figure 1: Average Scores of Top 100 Philippine Publicly Listed Companies by Market Capitalization, 2012–2016

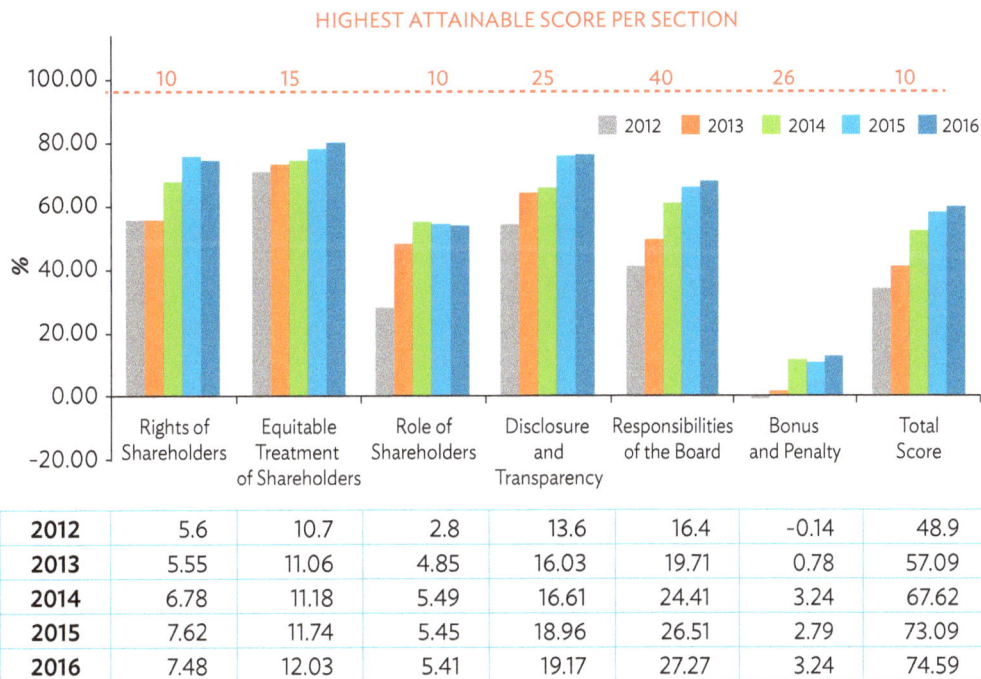

HIGHEST ATTAINABLE SCORE PER SECTION

	Rights of Shareholders	Equitable Treatment of Shareholders	Role of Shareholders	Disclosure and Transparency	Responsibilities of the Board	Bonus and Penalty	Total Score
2012	5.6	10.7	2.8	13.6	16.4	-0.14	48.9
2013	5.55	11.06	4.85	16.03	19.71	0.78	57.09
2014	6.78	11.18	5.49	16.61	24.41	3.24	67.62
2015	7.62	11.74	5.45	18.96	26.51	2.79	73.09
2016	7.48	12.03	5.41	19.17	27.27	3.24	74.59

Note: The graph shows the percentage equivalent of the raw scores in relation to the highest attainable score per section.

Source: Institute of Corporate Directors. 2018. *Philippine Results 2017 ACGS – ASEAN Corporate Governance Scorecard*. Primer prepared for the ACGS Appreciation Ceremony. Manila. 31 July.

The sections that require most attention and improvement are Role of Stakeholders (Part C) and Responsibilities of the Board (Part E). The average scores for both sections have seen some improvements from 2012–2016 but have also consistently remained the sections with the lowest scores throughout the 5 years of assessment. In 2015, the average score of Philippine PLCs in Part C (5.45) was lower than Thailand (8.09), Indonesia (6.96), Malaysia (6.70), and Singapore (5.70). Similarly, the average score of Philippine PLCs in Part E (26.51) is lower than the average score in most other ASEAN countries including Singapore (29.71), Thailand (29.68), and Malaysia (29.22). According to the 2015 report, one area for improvement in Part C of Philippine PLCs is providing specific contact details to stakeholders so that they can raise possible violations of their rights. General contact details typically found on company websites are insufficient. Commitment to stakeholders should be facilitated with easy communication. For Part E, areas that require improvement include: (i) the board should be composed of at least 50% independent directors, (ii) companies should have a policy that limits to five board seats in publicly listed companies that an independent or nonexecutive director may hold simultaneously, and (iii) companies should also have a term limit of 9 years or less for its independent directors (footnote 2). Some of these issues are already included in the Corporate Governance Blueprint of the Philippines (discussed below). Engagement on their importance and assessment of compliance will be important to prompt improvement.

1.3   Corporate Governance Philippine Regulatory Reform

In the years covered by the study, three key corporate governance policies were developed and implemented in the Philippines. First, in 2013, the SEC required all PLCs to issue an annual corporate governance report, which consolidated all their governance policies and practices into one report for easy reference. The report was mandatory and due to be submitted by June of every fiscal year. In addition, in October 2013, to improve transparency, the SEC required all PLCs to upload their annual corporate governance reports on their respective websites. Prior to this, disclosures by Philippine PLCs were not centralized: some information were posted on their websites, some were posted through the Philippine Stock Exchange, and some were disclosed through the SEC. As a result of this requirement, investors now have a one-stop reference for all disclosures of a PLC.

Second, in 2015, SEC published the Philippine Corporate Governance Blueprint to serve as a 5-year roadmap for building a stronger corporate governance framework. This initiative was supported by ADB and was developed through a robust process that combined using the OECD principles as reference point for international best practice and through consultation with local PLCs, governance advocates, academe, and corporate governance stakeholders. Using the globally accepted principles of corporate governance, the blueprint made the corporate governance regulatory framework geared not only toward compliance, but also toward addressing challenges faced by companies in the country.

Many of the recommendations contained in the blueprint are consistent with the best practices espoused by the ACGS, which include the following:

(i)   Release of the information statements 28 days before the annual shareholders meeting. Rationale and explanation of each agenda item that requires shareholders' approval should be provided.

(ii)   Right of shareholders to nominate candidates to the board. In publicly listed companies, full disclosure of the background and experience of the candidates to the board (including other board positions) is expected.

(iii)   Material or significant related party transactions (RPTs) and similar matters involving conflicts of interest should be disclosed fully, accurately, and in a timely fashion.

(iv)   Mechanisms enhancing employee performance are encouraged. Programs and relative information on the welfare and development of the employees should be available.

(v)   Companies should have a formal and transparent board nomination process. There should also be succession planning for key management positions.

(vi)   There should be a right mix of backgrounds and competencies in the board; thus, companies should have a board diversity policy and are encouraged to have female independent directors.[3]

---

[3]   Government of the Philippines, Securities and Exchange Commission. 2015. *Philippines Corporate Governance Blueprint 2015*. Manila.

Finally, in 2016, the SEC revised and issued the Corporate Governance Code for PLCs. This code encouraged and steered companies to apply practices at par with global standards in order to attract foreign investments. It also addressed the perceived "overregulation" of SEC by opting for a "comply or explain" approach, providing more flexibility for companies. This is a market-based approach that requires PLCs to disclosed non-compliance, which then relies on investors to provide feedback and challenge the management, if necessary.

The revised code focuses on five key areas:

(i)   the board's governance responsibilities,

(ii)   disclosure and transparency,

(iii)   internal control system and risk management framework,

(iv)   cultivating a synergistic relationship with shareholders, and

(v)   duties to stakeholders.

With 16 principles and 67 best practice recommendations, the code raised corporate governance standards of Philippine PLCs, and fostered a conducive governance system accountable to shareholders and stakeholders.

These policies, complemented with intense engagement led by SEC and ICD with the PLCs, contributed to the improvement in the average score of Philippine PLCs from 48.9 in 2012 to 74.6 in 2016, thus making the Philippines one of the most improved countries. In fact, in 2015, 11 Philippine PLCs were ranked in the top 50 ASEAN PLCs, which placed the Philippines second behind Thailand, which had 23 PLCs in the top 50.[4] This achievement demonstrated that Philippine PLCs are able to stand toe to toe with other PLCs in the ASEAN region and subscribe to international corporate governance best practices, contrary to the belief of some local stakeholders who felt that said international best practices would stifle innovation and entrepreneurship.

The improving performance of Philippine PLCs motivated the SEC to formulate policies that would further strengthen the governance framework and implementation by companies from various industries. In support of this effort, ICD undertook the quantitative assessment in the next section. After 5 years assessing corporate governance practices, ICD felt the need to evaluate the impact of the ACGS scores on the financial performance of Philippine PLCs.

---

[4] While these 11 PLCs did well, the average score of all Philippines PLCs assessed were still behind the average score of PLCs in Thailand, Singapore, and Malaysia.

2. RESEARCH PROBLEM

The study sought to determine the impact of the quality of corporate governance practices on the market capitalization, market valuation, and profitability of publicly listed companies (PLCs) in the Philippines.

3. OBJECTIVES OF THE STUDY

The study aims to

(i)   measure the quality of corporate governance practices of Philippine PLCs using the ASEAN Corporate Governance Scorecard (ACGS) score,

(ii)   measure the market capitalization of Philippine PLCs using data from the Philippine Stock Exchange (PSE),

(iii)   measure the market valuation of Philippine PLCs using the Tobin's Q ratio,

(iv)   measure the profitability of Philippine PLCs using the return on equity ratio,

(v)   determine the relationship between ACGS score and market capitalization of Philippine PLCs,

(vi)   determine the relationship between ACGS score and Tobin's Q ratio of Philippine PLCs, and

(vii)   determine the relationship between ACGS score and the return on equity ratio of Philippine PLCs.

The results of the study will be used to help resolve issues regarding the financial benefits of good corporate governance practices. They will serve to inform board directors, compliance officers, and corporate secretaries of Philippine PLCs as well as regulators, investors, and other stakeholders.

4. REVIEW OF RELATED STUDIES

Studies have been conducted on the relation between corporate governance and the financial performance of a firm in both developed and emerging markets. Some of these studies used an index to measure the overall corporate governance practices of companies. Other studies considered the relationship of specific aspects of corporate governance on firm performance. There are studies that provided evidence on the benefits of adopting good corporate governance practices. There are also studies that presented opposing conclusions on the relation between corporate governance practices and firm performance.

Khanna (2016) used secondary data taken from the annual reports of publicly listed companies from the Indian manufacturing sector for the period 2011 to 2015. These companies were from the consumable goods, fast-moving consumer goods, pharmaceutical, and automobile sectors. The study measured the corporate governance practices of the manufacturing sector of India, and the relationship between corporate governance and the profitability of the manufacturing companies. The study considered the relationship between each corporate governance parameter given in the Securities and Exchange Board of India (SEBI) clause 49 of the listing agreement and return on assets, a measure of profitability. The seven parameters given in the SEBI clause 49 of the listing agreement are as follows:

(i)   board composition,

(ii)   shareholding pattern,

(iii)   board level committee,

(iv)   audit committee,

(v)   number of subsidiaries,

(vi)   disclosures, and

(vii) other compliance.

The secondary data were analyzed using correlation analysis and multiple regression analysis. The dependent variable is return on assets or profit before tax and interest divided by total assets. The independent variables are the seven parameters of corporate governance.

The results showed that the level of corporate governance among the Indian manufacturing companies is high. The findings also showed that four parameters of corporate governance—board composition, board ownership or shareholding pattern, disclosures, and other compliance—have a positive and significant impact on the profitability of Indian manufacturing companies. The study concluded that better corporate governance can lead to higher profitability.

Cheung et al. (2014) investigated the relation between the quality of corporate governance practices and market valuation for listed firms in five Asian ADB member economies: Hong Kong, China; Indonesia; the People's Republic of China; the Philippines, and Thailand. The study used a survey instrument that is based on the OECD Corporate Governance Principles (OECD, 1999), which cover five aspects of corporate governance (rights of shareholders, treatment of shareholders, roles of shareholders, disclosure and transparency, and board responsibilities). The survey quantified the quality of corporate governance practices through a Corporate Governance Index (CGI) value for each company, which ranges from 0 to 100. High CGI scores indicate good corporate governance practices while low CGI scores indicate poor corporate governance practices. The study used Tobin's Q ratio as the measure of firm market valuation. Tobin's Q ratio was defined in the study as the sum of the market value of equity plus book value of total interest-bearing debt divided by the sum of the book value of equity plus the book value of total debt. Market value was the market value of shareholders' equity (in millions, in local currency). The ordinary least squares regression model used control variables: firm size (natural logarithm of the book value of total assets in local currency at the end of the fiscal year), leverage (total interest-bearing debt divided by total assets), liquidity (the balance sheet value of cash and cash equivalents divided by total assets), and the level of investment (capital expenditures divided by total assets). Variables to indicate the survey year are also included as a year fixed effect.

The study used annual publicly available information from publicly traded firms to rate the corporate governance practices of the major companies in each of the stock markets. The empirical results showed that there is a positive relation between the quality of corporate governance practices as measured by the CGI and firm valuation in the five countries. To verify the robustness of the findings, the study used two-stage least squares regression analyses to check on whether well-performing firms tend to improve their corporate governance practices. The results confirm the positive relation between the quality of corporate governance practices and firm valuation.

Klapper and Love (2003) examined the relationship between the CGI score and firm performance for 374 firms in 14 emerging markets. The results showed that better corporate governance practices among emerging markets is highly correlated with better operating performance and market valuation. The study likewise provided evidence showing that firm-level corporate governance practices matter more in countries with weak legal environments. The results showed that firm-level governance and performance is lower in countries with weak legal environments i.e., weak shareholder rights and inefficient enforcement.

The data for the study came from the Credit Lyonnais Securities Asia (CLSA) 2001 report, which provided corporate governance rankings for 495 firms across 25 emerging markets and 18 sectors. The descriptive statistics in the CLSA report showed that companies which got high rankings in the CGI had better operating performance and higher stock returns. The governance index covers seven categories: management discipline, transparency, independence, accountability, responsibility, fairness, and social awareness.

Klapper and Love (2003) used multivariate regression analysis to further investigate the relationship between governance and performance. They used the computed governance index of CLSA as the independent variable, although they excluded the social awareness category. They used Tobin's Q ratio and return on assets (ROA) as dependent variables. Tobin's Q ratio was used to measure the market valuation of assets and ROA was used to measure operating performance. ROA was defined as net income over total assets. They also used other measures of operating performance such as gross margin and return on equity.

The results showed that better corporate governance is associated with higher operating performance and that the CGI is higher in countries with good legal environments.

Bhagat and Bolton (2007) sought to provide a comprehensive and "econometrically-defensible" analysis of the relation between corporate governance and firm performance. The authors used a total of 24 metrics composed of nine governance metrics, five performance metrics, two endogenous metrics, and eight control variables. The study covered a period of 15 years (from 1990 to 2004) with the sample size reaching up to 25,000.

A series of robustness tests was also conducted to check the soundness of the statistical model and corresponding assumptions. The tests included the validity and strength of instruments used, assessment of variable estimators, estimation of standard errors, and alternate measures of leverage.

The Bhagat and Bolton (2007) study found that good corporate governance was positively and significantly correlated with operating performance. However, none of the governance metrics are correlated with stock market performance.

5. CONCEPTUAL FRAMEWORK

The study reported here is modeled after Cheung et al. (2014) with a number of additions and variations. The market capitalization of the firm is added as a dependent variable. Return on equity as a metric of profitability is also added as a dependent variable. Finally, the formula for Tobin's Q is simplified given the available data.

The independent variable for the study is the ACGS score of Philippine PLCs for the years 2014, 2015, and 2016. The dependent variables are market capitalization (stock price multiplied by number of shares outstanding as supplied by the Philippine Stock Exchange), Tobin's Q ratio (equity market value divided by equity book value), and return on equity or ROE (net income divided by the shareholders' equity).[5] The organizational factors are the control variables: firm size (natural logarithm of the book value of total assets in local currency at the end of the fiscal year), leverage (total liabilities divided by the shareholders' equity), liquidity (the balance sheet value of cash and cash equivalents divided by total assets), and the level of investment (fixed assets divided by total assets and net income divided by common equity). Variables to indicate the survey year are also included as a year fixed effect.

---

[5] The simplified version of the Tobin's Q ratio used in the study can be found in Investopedia at *https://www.investopedia. com/terms/q/qratio.asp.*

6. METHODOLOGY

6.1   Scope and Limitation

The study sample consists of 73 PLCs, each of which had an ACGS score of 60 points or higher in the years 2014, 2015, and 2016. The cutoff score was imposed in the sample selection based on the observation by the study team that a company with a score of 60 or higher tends to have a conscious and deliberate effort to comply with the governance requirements of the ACGS; hence, the achievement of good financial performance is not a random occurrence. The excluded PLCs were also seen to be outliers in the data set that could potentially cause "non-normality" in the results. In view of these limitations, regression with the panel-corrected standard errors (PCSE) was used to reduce the effect of the limitations.

Of the three dependent variables, the study puts an emphasis on market valuation indicated by Tobin's Q. Tobin's Q ratio follows the hypothesis that the aggregate equity market value of all companies in the stock market should be about equal to their replacement costs. Calculated by dividing the equity market value of the firm by its equity book value, the Q ratio serves as a method of firm valuation by showing whether a firm is overvalued or undervalued by the market. A Q ratio value between 0 and 1 means that the firm's perceived value in the market is lower than its total asset value. On the other hand, a Q ratio value of greater than 1 means that the market has placed a premium value on the firm more than the equity book value it possesses.

6.2   Research Design and Data Analysis

The methodology used in the study was adopted generally from the study of Cheung et al. (2014). Descriptive statistics (i.e., mean and standard deviation) were computed for the independent, dependent, and control variables of each company for each year. Regression with PCSE was used to examine the relationship between the ACGS score and market capitalization, between the ACGS score and Tobin's Q ratio, and between the ACGS score and return on equity ratio.

The PCSE model used control variables: firm size (natural logarithm of the book value of total assets in local currency at the end of the fiscal year), leverage (total liabilities divided by the shareholders' equity), liquidity (balance sheet value of cash and cash equivalents divided by total assets), and the level of investment (capital expenditures divided by total assets). Variables to indicate the survey year are also included as a year fixed effect.

To verify the robustness of the findings, the study used two-stage least squares regression analyses to check on whether well-performing firms tend to improve their corporate governance practices.

7. COLLABORATION

This study was undertaken by ICD Philippines with the assistance of ADB using annual data pertaining to years 2014, 2015, and 2016. Statistical, methodological support and peer review was provided by the University of Asia and the Pacific.

8. OVERALL FINDINGS

Table 1: Descriptive Statistics

Description (1)	Year (2)	Tobin's Q (3)	ACGS Score (4)	Market Capitalization [₱ billion] (5)	ROE (6)	Size (7)	Leverage (8)	Liquidity (9)	Level of Investments (10)	Sample Size (11)
Mean	2014	2.16	75.02	110.44	0.10	24.56	2.37	0.50	0.66	73
	2015	1.81	81.48	106.77	0.08	24.64	2.43	0.10	3.27	73
	2016	1.80	83.19	112.01	0.10	24.85	2.64	0.09	0.29	73
	All years	1.92	79.90	109.74	0.09	24.68	2.48	0.23	1.41	219
Standard Deviation	2014	2.02	11.48	156.45	0.12	2.14	2.59	3.33	3.14	73
	2015	1.81	13.78	160.36	0.20	2.22	2.64	0.13	24.68	73
	2016	1.77	15.51	169.95	0.09	2.12	2.71	0.10	0.23	73
	All years	1.87	14.08	161.62	0.14	2.15	2.64	1.93	14.36	219

ACGS = ASEAN Corporate Governance Scorecard, ROE = return on equity.

Notes:
(a) This table presents the descriptive statistics of the sample. It shows the means and standard deviations of the variables given in columns 3–10, which are provided specifically for each of the 3 years included in the study, i.e., 2014, 2015, and 2016, and for all years.
(b) The "All years" figures represent the means and standard deviations of the variables in columns 3–10, and are each the average for the 3-year period for that specific column.
(c) The descriptive results showed that the average Tobin's Q ratio (column 3) for each year and all years were consistently above 1.0. Theoretically, Tobin's Q ratio with a value above 1.0 indicates that the firm's equity market value is worth more than its equity book value.
(d) In this study, the average Tobin's Q ratio of the firms included in the study was highest in 2014 (2.16), while 2015 and 2016 posted almost the same values.

Source: Processed data from company annual reports and the Philippine Stock Exchange (2014-2016).

Table 1 shows the average and the extent of variation within the data set of the variables used in the study for each of the years 2014, 2015, and 2016, as well as for the combined 3-year period.[6] The ACGS scores of the companies in the sample increased from 2014 to 2016, a clear indication of continuous improvement in corporate governance practices. This could indicate that companies are motivated to further enhance their corporate governance efforts through time. However, the Tobin's Q ratio indicating firm valuation appeared to have an inverse effect with 2014 having the highest mean value and 2015 to 2016 lagging behind. One probable explanation for this counterintuitive observation lies not so much on firm performance but more on the stock market performance.

The Philippine stock market had a good year in 2014, rising by 22.66% by the end of the year. However, the steady rise of the market ended in the middle of 2015, followed by a continuous downtrend which ended with the stock market down by 3.9% upon its closing. In 2016, the Philippine stock market faced a volatile year with its rise attributed to positive economic outlook and infrastructure investment by the new Philippine administration, and its decline attributed to fears surrounding the US Federal Government rate hike, falling oil prices, and the incumbent US administration's tirade against international institutions in industrialized countries. By the end of 2016, the market was down by 1.6%.

As the overall sentiment in the stock market directly affects the share price of individual companies, it would have, by extension, also affected their Tobin's Q ratio. This would account for the decreasing Tobin's Q ratio averages over the 2014 to 2016 period. In this case, the improvement of ACGS practices might have been nullified by the decline in stock market performance. The same explanation would apply for the fluctuations in the market capitalization of individual companies over the same period.

Average firm size did not show as much year-to-year variation. On the other hand, values of mean leverage showed that companies had more liabilities than their shareholders' equity, but it showed a rather stable increasing trend during the covered period. The patterns of the values concerning liquidity and level of investment also exhibited a fluctuating pattern similar to the other variables.

To measure the relationship between corporate governance and the market capitalization of publicly listed companies in the Philippines.

$$MC_{it} = \beta_0 + \beta_1 CG\_Score_{it} + \beta_2 Size_{it} + \beta_3 Leverage_{it} + \beta_4 Liquidity_{it} + \beta_5 Level\ of\ Investments_{it} + \sigma_1 T_1 + \sigma_2 T_2 + \sigma_3 T_3 + \alpha_i + \varepsilon_{it}$$

(1)

---

[6] In this study, the average Tobin's Q ratio of the firms was highest in 2014 (2.16), while 2015 and 2016 posted almost the same values.

Table 2: Panel-Corrected Standard Errors for ACGS Score and Market Capitalization Regression Results

| | Model 1 | |
	Coefficient	P-value
ACGS score	3.032	0.000***
Size	45.569	0.000***
Leverage	-17.064	0.000***
Liquidity	2.028	0.427
Level of investments	1.090	0.164
Year 2015	-27.744	0.000***
Year 2016	-30.266	0.000***
Intercept	-1197.621	0.000***
Wald chi^2	5738.60	
Prob > chi^2		0.000***
No. of observations = 219		
No. of groups = 73		

ACGS = ASEAN Corporate Governance Scorecard.

Notes:
(a) Market capitalization is the market value of shareholders' equity (in billions and in Philippine pesos). Control variables included size, leverage, liquidity, and investments. Size is the log of total assets. Leverage denotes the debt ratio (total liabilities divided by the shareholders' equity). Liquidity is the ratio of cash and cash equivalents to assets while the investments variable is the ratio of capital expenditures to total assets. Panel data is strongly balanced. Year 2014 is the reference year; thus, it is omitted in the results.
(b) *** indicates significant @99% confidence level.

Source: From the results of the regression analysis done by the researchers from University of Asia and the Pacific.

The results as shown in Table 2 showed that the ACGS score has a positive and highly significant effect on the market capitalization, after controlling for time-fixed-effects and firm-specific differences such as size, leverage, liquidity, and level of investments. The results of this study suggest that an increase in the ACGS score by one unit will also increase the predicted market capitalization (in billions) by 3.032 when all other things remain constant. This likely suggests that the efforts and resources put in by the corporations in increasing their ACGS scores are paid off with an increased market capitalization.

To measure the relationship between corporate governance and the market valuation of publicly listed companies in the Philippines.

$$q_{it} = \beta_0 + \beta_1 CG\_Score_{it} + \beta_2 Size_{it} + \beta_3 Leverage_{it} + \beta_4 Liquidity_{it} + \beta_5 Investments_{it} + \sigma_1 T_1 + \sigma_2 T_2 + \sigma_3 T_{3+} u_{it}$$

(2)

$$CG\_Score_{it} = \beta_0 + \beta_1 q_{it} + \beta_2 Size_{it} + \beta_3 Leverage_{it} + + \beta_4 Liquidity_{it} + \beta_5 Investments_{it} + \sigma_1 T_1 + \sigma_2 T_2 + \sigma_3 T_3 + \alpha_i + \varepsilon_{it}$$

(3)

Table 3: **Panel-Corrected Standard Errors for ACGS Score and Market Valuation Two-Stage Regression Results**

| | Model 2 | | Model 3 | |
| | Tobin's Q | | ACGS Score | |
	Coefficient	P-value	Coefficient	P-value
ACGS score	0.027	0.006***		
Tobin's Q			1.010	0.007***
Size	-0.117	0.004***	3.898	0.000***
Leverage	-0.040	0.015**	-0.494	0.035**
Liquidity	-0.069	0.000***	0.815	0.000***
Level of investments	0.006	0.181	0.057	0.243
Year 2015	-0.511	0.000***	6.709	0.000***
Year 2016	-0.561	0.000***	7.911	0.000***
Intercept	3.103	0.000***	-22.175	0.087
Wald Chi^2	148.83		3574.56	
Prob > Chi^2		0.000***		0.000***
No. of observations = 219				
No. of groups = 73				

ACGS = ASEAN Corporate Governance Scorecard, PCSE = panel-corrected standard errors.

Notes:
(a) The dependent variable in model 2 is Tobin's Q ratio, while the dependent variable in model 3 is ACGS scores. The Tobin's Q ratio was used as proxy for the market valuation. Models 2 and 3 both employed regression with PCSE so that estimations of results are robust to data disturbances.
(b) Tobin's Q ratio in this study is defined as the market value of equity divided by the book value of equity. Controlling variables include size, leverage, liquidity, level of investments, and time-effects. For the time-effects, reference year is 2014 that is why Stata omitted the results for 2014.
(c) *** indicates significant @99% confidence level, ** indicates significant @ 95% confidence level.

Source: From the results of the regression analysis done by the researchers from University of Asia and the Pacific.

Table 3 shows that in model 2, Hausman specification test and Breusch and Pagan LM test both suggested the use of Random-effects GLS panel regression, yet model 2 suffers from the presence of heteroskedasticity, autocorrelation, and cross-sectional dependence. Thus, the PCSE was again employed with time dummies considering that upon testing for time-effects, results suggested that controlling for time-effects is needed. For model 3, Hausman test suggested the use of fixed-effects over random-effects. However, just like the case of model 2, model 3 also suffered the same data disturbances and the need to control for time-fixed-effects. Hence, model 3 also employed regression with PCSE and with time dummies. On one hand, the Prob>chi2 of models 2 and 3 were both less than 0.05, which suggest that the models are acceptable and that all coefficients in the models are different from zero.

The results for model 2 showed that there is a positive and highly significant relationship between ACGS score as a proxy for quality of corporate governance practices and the market valuation as measured by Tobin's Q ratio after controlling for time-effects and the firm-specific differences such as size, leverage, liquidity, and level of investments. The results demonstrate that an increase in ACGS score by one unit will also increase the Tobin's Q ratio by 0.027, keeping everything else constant.

This suggests that efforts and resources put in by the corporations in increasing their ACGS scores are matched by an increase in the predicted value of their Tobin's Q ratio. In the same way, results for model 3 also showed that there is a positive and highly significant relationship between Tobin's Q ratio and ACGS score after controlling for time-effects and firm-specific differences. Results in models 2 and 3 suggest that increasing the ACGS score will increase Tobin's Q ratio, and vice versa.

To measure the relationship between corporate governance and the profitability of publicly listed companies in the Philippines.

$$ROE_{it} = \beta_0 + \beta_1 CG\ Score_{it} + \beta_2 Size_{it} + \beta_3 Leverage_{it} + \beta_4 Liquidity_{it} + \beta_5 Investments_{it} + u_{it}$$

(4)

Table 4: Panel-Corrected Standard Errors for ACGS Score and Return on Equity Regression Results

	Model 4	
	Coefficient	P-value
ACGS score	0.003	0.002***
Size	0.011	0.005***
Leverage	–0.012	0.001***
Liquidity	–0.000	0.917
Level of investments	–0.000	0.216
Intercept	–0.345	0.000***
Wald Chi²	213.87	
Prob > chi²		0.000***
No. of observations = 219		
No. of groups = 73		

ACGS = ASEAN Corporate Governance Scorecard, ASEAN = Association of Southeast Asian Nations.

Notes:

(a) The dependent variable in this model is return on equity as a measure of profitability, which is measured as the firm's net income divided by the firm's equity at book value. Controlling variables include size, leverage, liquidity, and investments.

(b) *** indicates significant @99% confidence level.

Source: From the results of the regression analysis done by the researchers from University of Asia and the Pacific.

Results showed that the coefficient of ACGS score is positive and highly significant, although the absolute increase in value could be considered minimal. Nonetheless, the results imply that increasing the quality of corporate governance practices would result in an increase (although minimal) on the return on equity (ROE) as a measure of profitability after controlling for firm-specific differences. The results point out that an increase in ACGS score by one unit would increase the ROE by 0.003 when all other things remain constant.

Again, results of models 1 to 4 showed that companies that enhance efforts and resources to raise the quality of their corporate governance—as reflected in increasing ACGS scores—would experience a positive impact on their market capitalization, market valuation, and profitability, after controlling for firm-specific differences and time-effects, if needed.

In Figure 2, the distances between data points are narrow and more compact near the corporate governance score threshold. As the ACGS score increases, the points become more dispersed and would show corresponding increase and growth in the market capitalization. It is also probable that companies with large market capitalization would have resources to effectively implement better corporate governance practices, hence their correlation.

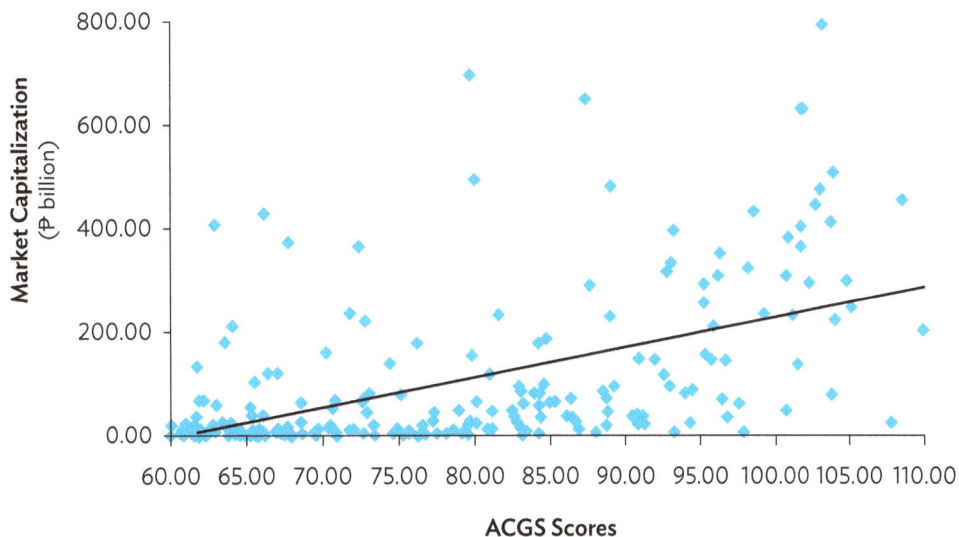

Figure 2: **ASEAN Corporate Governance Scorecard Scores versus Market Capitalization** (₱ billion)

ACGS = ASEAN Corporate Governance Scorecard, ICD = Institute of Corporate Directors, PLC = publicly listed company.

Notes:
(a) This figure shows a scatter plot of ACGS score and market capitalization of the sample PLCs.
(b) In a number of instances, those with a high ACGS score also have a high market capitalization (expressed in billion pesos).
(c) However, there are also cases where companies have a high ACGS score but their market capitalization is not commensurately high.

Source: Data was obtained from the published reports of PLCs uploaded in the online database of the Philippine Stock Exchange and the ACGS assessments done by ICD Philippines.

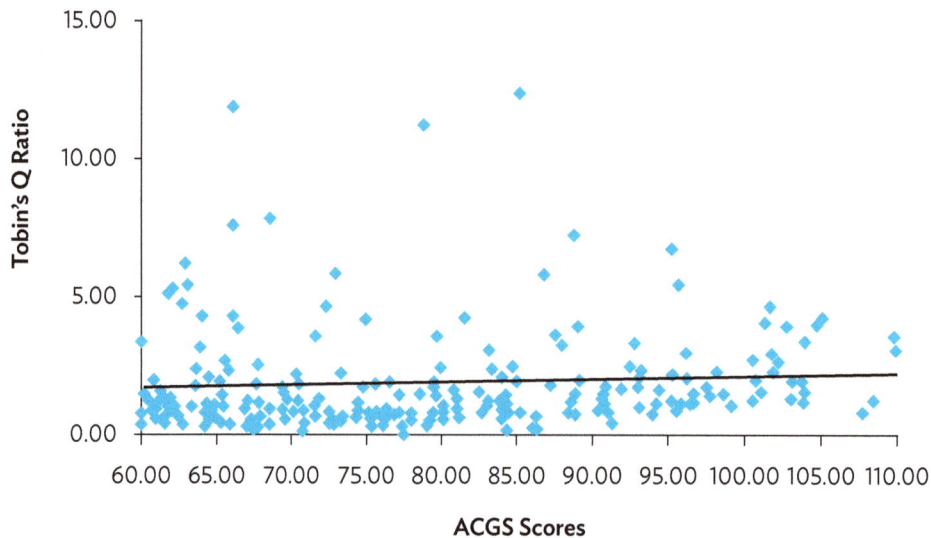

Figure 3: ASEAN Corporate Governance Scorecard Scores versus Tobin's Q Ratio

ACGS = ASEAN Corporate Governance Scorecard, ICD = Institute of Corporate Directors, PLC = publicly listed company

Note: This figure also shows a scatter plot where some companies have a high ACGS score but a low Tobin's Q ratio. At same time, there are companies which have a low ACGS score but a high Tobin's Q ratio.

Source: Data was obtained from the published reports of PLCs uploaded in the online database of the Philippine Stock Exchange and the ACGS assessments done by ICD Philippines.

In Figure 3, the Tobin's Q ratios of firms with ACGS scores on the higher end of the spectrum exhibit similarly low values as firms with lower ACGS scores.[7] The continuous decline of the Philippine stock market performance in 2015 and 2016 may have contributed to the lower than expected values of Tobin's Q ratio and the absence of a distinctive upward trend between the two variables. Another probable explanation is the lack of awareness and appreciation by investors of the ACGS scores or governance practices of companies, as well as the influence of these factors on firm valuation. It should be noted the ACGS scores, and the quality of governance practices they represent, are still not openly disclosed or publicized for individual PLCs.

---

[7]   Based on the results of model 2, an increase by one unit of ACGS score will increase the Tobin's Q ratio by 0.027, if all other factors remain constant, with a confidence level of 99%.

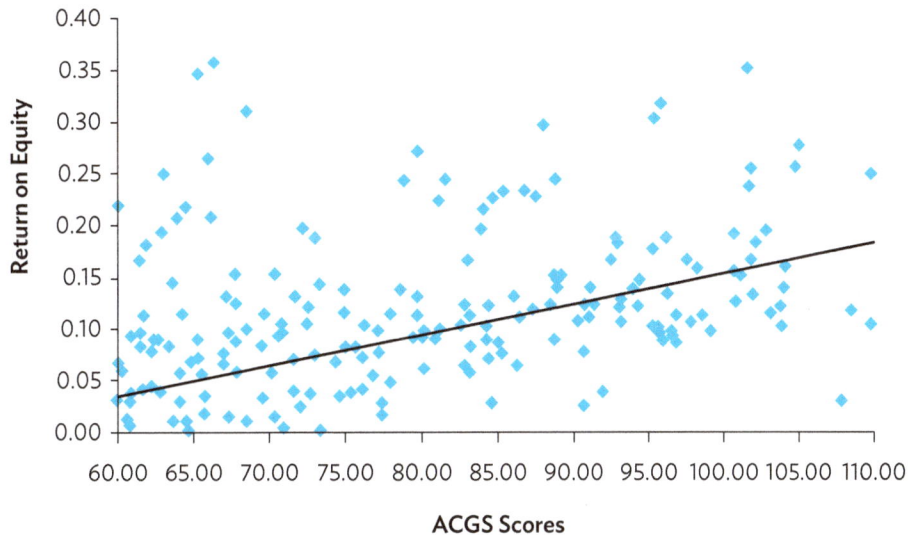

Figure 4: **ASEAN Corporate Governance Scorecard Scores versus Return on Equity**

ACGS = ASEAN Corporate Governance Scorecard, ICD = Institute of Corporate Directors, PLC = publicly listed company, ROE = return on equity.

Note: This figure shows a scatter plot of ACGS scores and ROE values of the sample publicly listed companies. One might find it difficult to infer on the trend considering that some companies had a negative ROE, but their ACGS score was higher than some other companies with a positive ROE. Nonetheless, most companies had a positive ROE.

Source: Data was obtained from the published reports of PLCs uploaded in the online database of the Philippine Stock Exchange and the ACGS assessments done by ICD Philippines.

Removing the negative outlier from Figure 4, the data points appear to be fairly dispersed from the regression line.[8] Using statistical correlation tests, the ACGS scores appear to have a weak linear correlation to the ROE of firms. The dispersion of data points also shows wide variances from the trend or regression.

---

[8] Again, based on the results in Table 5, the correlation between ACGS score and ROE is considered to be positive, but a weak linear relationship with a correlation coefficient of 0.2993.

Table 5: **Correlation Matrix of Variables**

	ACGS Score	Market Capitalization [billions]	Tobin's Q Ratio	Return on Equity	Firm Size	Leverage	Liquidity Ratio	Level of Investments
ACGS Score	1.0000							
Market Capitalization [billions]	0.5268	1.0000						
Tobin's Q Ratio	0.0937	0.2587	1.0000					
Return on Equity	0.2993	0.2496	0.2839	1.0000				
Firm Size	0.5384	0.6041	-0.0444	0.1829	1.0000			
Leverage	0.1935	0.0722	-0.0828	-0.0971	0.5082	1.0000		
Liquidity Ratio	0.0040	-0.0232	-0.0225	-0.0076	-0.1630	-0.1092	1.0000	
Level of Investments	0.1137	0.1634	0.0516	0.0188	0.0448	-0.0327	0.1192	1.0000

ACGS = ASEAN Corporate Governance Scorecard.

Source: From the results of the regression analysis done by the researchers from University of Asia and the Pacific.

9. CONCLUSION

The Institute of Corporate Directors (ICD) defines corporate governance as "the system by which companies are directed and controlled by a board of directors, acting collegially." The corporate governance of ASEAN publicly listed companies (PLCs) is evaluated using the ASEAN Corporate Governance Scorecard (ACGS), a benchmarking tool based on international best practices.

The Philippines' performance in the ACGS steadily rose from its assessment in 2012 through 2016. After years of experience with the ACGS, ICD saw the need and opportunity to explore the impact of corporate governance practices on the financial performance and market perception of Philippine PLCs. Thus, the study sought to determine how and to what extent the quality of corporate governance practices, as measured by the ACGS, relate to the market capitalization, market valuation, and profitability of PLCs.

The study is intended to help resolve issues regarding the financial benefits of good corporate governance practices. Its results will inform board directors, compliance officers, and corporate secretaries of Philippine PLCs, as well as regulators, investors, and other stakeholders.

A review of literature identified past studies that attempted to establish the relationship between corporate governance and financial performance of a firm in both developed and emerging markets. Some of these studies used an overall corporate governance index to measure the overall corporate governance practices of companies. Other studies considered the relationship of specific aspects of corporate governance on firm performance. There are studies that provided evidence of the benefits of adopting good corporate governance practices. There are also studies that presented opposing conclusions on the relation between corporate governance practices and firm performance.

The methodology of this current study was modeled after that of Cheung et al. (2014). Descriptive statistics (i.e., mean and standard deviation) were computed for the independent, dependent, and control variables of companies in a sample of 73 PLCs and for each of the 3 years (2014, 2015, and 2016) covered by the study. Regression with panel-corrected standard errors (PCSE) was used to examine the relationship between the ACGS score and market capitalization, between the ACGS score and Tobin's Q ratio, and between the ACGS score and return on equity ratio.

The results of the study showed that for the group of PLCs included in the study, there is a positive and statistically significant relationship between (i) corporate governance and market capitalization, (ii) corporate governance and market valuation as measured by Tobin's Q ratio, and (iii) corporate governance and profitability as measured by return on equity. This means that as the quality of corporate governance practices improves, it is likely that firm market capitalization, market valuation, and profitability will increase as well.

The study indicates that increasing the efforts and resources devoted to improving the quality of corporate governance practices of a PLC would create positive and significant effects on its market capitalization, market valuation, and profitability. Thus, it is worthwhile for PLCs to work on raising the quality of their corporate governance practices and, in the process, improve their ACGS score. Regulations that go beyond compliance can help raise the bar on corporate governance in the country.

On the buy side of the market, institutional and other investors in the country must be afforded access to the results of the ACGS process so they can reward PLCs with high governance scores with appropriate premiums on their share price.

REFERENCES

ASEAN Capital Markets Forum and Asian Development Bank. 2013. *ASEAN Corporate Governance Scorecard: Country Reports and Assessments 2012–2013.*

———. 2014. *ASEAN Corporate Governance Scorecard: Country Reports and Assessments 2013–2014.*

———. 2017. *ASEAN Corporate Governance Scorecard: Country Reports and Assessments 2015.*

Bhagat, S. and B. Bolton. 2007. *Corporate Governance and Firm Performance.*

Cheung, Y. et al. 2014. Corporate Governance and Firm Valuation in Asian Emerging Markets. In Boubaker, S. and D.K. Nguyen, eds. 2014. *Corporate Governance in Emerging Markets: Theories, Practices and Cases.* NY: Springer-Verlag Berlin Heidelberg. pp. 27–53.

Government of the Philippines, Securities and Exchange Commission. 2015. Philippines Corporate Governance Blueprint 2015. Manila.

Institute of Corporate Directors. 2018. Philippine Results 2017 ACGS–ASEAN Corporate Governance Scorecard. Primer prepared for the ACGS Appreciation Ceremony. Manila. 31 July.

Khanna, V. 2016. Corporate Governance and Performance: Indian Manufacturing Sector. *SCMS Journal of Indian Management.* July–September. pp. 33–45.

Klapper, L. F. and I. Love. 2003. Corporate Governance, Investor Protection, and Performance in Emerging Markets. *Journal of Corporate Finance.* 195. pp. 1–26.

ANNEXES

Annex 1: ASEAN Corporate Governance Scorecard

LEVEL 1

A. The Rights of Shareholders

A.1	Basic Shareholder Rights	Guiding Reference
A.1.1	Does the company pay (interim and final/annual) dividends in an equitable and timely manner; that is, all shareholders are treated equally and paid within 30 days after being (i) declared for interim dividends and (ii) approved by shareholders at general meetings for final dividends?	**OECD Principle II: The Rights of Shareholders and Key Ownership Functions** (A) Basic shareholder rights should include the right to, amongst others: (6) share in the profits of the corporation.

A.2	Right to participate in decisions concerning fundamental corporate changes.	Guiding Reference
Do shareholders have the right to participate in:		
A.2.1	Amendments to the company's constitution?	**OECD Principle II:** (B) Shareholders should have the right to participate in, and to be sufficiently informed on, decisions concerning fundamental corporate changes such as: (1) amendments to the statutes, or articles of incorporation or similar governing documents of the company.
A.2.2	The authorisation of additional shares?	**OECD Principle II (B):** (2) the authorisation of additional shares.
A.2.3	The transfer of all or substantially all assets, which in effect results in the sale of the company?	**OECD Principle II (B):** (3) extraordinary transactions, including the transfer of all or substantially all assets that in effect result in the sale of the company.

A.3	Right to participate effectively in and vote in general shareholder meetings and should be informed of the rules, including voting procedures that govern general shareholder meetings.	Guiding Reference
A.3.1	Do shareholders have the opportunity, evidenced by an agenda item, to approve remuneration (fees, allowances, benefit-in-kind and other emoluments) or any increases in remuneration for the non-executive directors/commissioners?	**OECD Principle II (C):** (3) Effective shareholder participation in key corporate governance decisions, such as the nomination and election of board members, should be facilitated. Shareholders should be able to make their views known on the remuneration policy for board members and key executives. The equity component of compensation schemes for board members and employees should be subject to shareholder approval.
A.3.2	Does the company provide non-controlling shareholders a right to nominate candidates for board of directors/commissioners?	
A.3.3	Does the company allow shareholders to elect directors/commissioners individually?	
A.3.4	Does the company disclose the voting and vote tabulation procedures used, declaring both before the meeting proceeds?	**OECD Principle II (C):** Shareholders should have the opportunity to participate effectively and vote in general shareholder meetings and should be informed of the rules, including voting procedures that govern general shareholder meetings.
A.3.5	Do the minutes of the most recent AGM record that there was an opportunity allowing for shareholders to ask questions or raise issues?	**OECD Principle II (C):** (2) Shareholders should have the opportunity to ask questions to the board, including questions relating to the annual external audit, to place items on the agenda of general meetings, and to propose resolutions, subject to reasonable limitations.
A.3.6	Do the minutes of the most recent AGM record questions and answers?	
A.3.7	Does the disclosure of the outcome of the most recent AGM include resolution(s)?	
A.3.8	Does the company disclose the voting results including approving, dissenting, and abstaining votes for each agenda item for the most recent AGM?	
A.3.9	Does the company disclose the list of board members who attended the most recent AGM?	**OECD Principle II (C); and ICGN 2.4.2:** All directors need to be able to allocate sufficient time to the board to perform their responsibilities effectively, including allowing some leeway for occasions when greater than usual time demands are made.
A.3.10	Did the chairman of the board of directors/commissioners attend the most recent AGM?	
A.3.11	Did the CEO/Managing Director/President attend the most recent AGM?	
A.3.12	Did the chairman of the Audit Committee attend the most recent AGM?	

A.3	Right to participate effectively in and vote in general shareholder meetings and should be informed of the rules, including voting procedures that govern general shareholder meetings.	Guiding Reference
A.3.13	Did the company organise their most recent AGM in an easy to reach location?	**OECD Principle II (C)**
A.3.14	Does the company allow for voting in absentia?	**OECD Principle II (C):** (4) Shareholders should be able to vote in person or in absentia, and equal effect should be given to votes whether cast in person or in absentia.
A.3.15	Did the company vote by poll (as opposed to by show of hands) for all resolutions at the most recent AGM?	**OECD Principle II (C)**
A.3.16	Does the company disclose that it has appointed an independent party (scrutinizers/inspectors) to count and/or validate the votes at the AGM?	
A.3.17	Does the company make publicly available by the next working day the result of the votes taken during the most recent AGM for all resolutions?	**OECD Principle II (C):** (1) Shareholders should be furnished with sufficient and timely information concerning the date, location and agenda of general meetings, as well as full and timely information regarding the issues to be decided at the meeting.
A.3.18	Do companies provide at least 21 days' notice for all resolutions?	
A.3.19	Does the company provide the rationale and explanation for each agenda item which require shareholders' approval in the notice of AGM/circulars and/or the accompanying statement?	

A.4	Markets for corporate control should be allowed to function in an efficient and transparent manner.	Guiding Reference
A.4.1	In cases of mergers, acquisitions and/or takeovers requiring shareholders' approval, does the board of directors/commissioners of the offeree company appoint an independent party to evaluate the fairness of the transaction price?	**OECD Principle II (E):** Markets for corporate control should be allowed to function in an efficient and transparent manner. (1) The rules and procedures governing the acquisition of corporate control in the capital markets, and extraordinary transactions such as mergers, and sales of substantial portions of corporate assets, should be clearly articulated and disclosed so that investors understand their rights and recourse. Transactions should occur at transparent prices and under fair conditions that protect the rights of all shareholders according to their class.

A.5	The exercise of ownership rights by all shareholders, including institutional investors, should be facilitated.	Guiding Reference
A.5.1	Does the Company publicly disclose policy/practice to encourage shareholders including institutional shareholders to attend the general meetings or engagement with the Company?	OECD Principle II (F): The exercise of ownership rights by all shareholders, including institutional investors, should be facilitated.

B.   Equitable Treatment of Shareholders

B.1	Shares and voting rights	Guiding Reference
B.1.1	Do the company's ordinary or common shares have one vote for one share?	OECD Principle III: (A) All shareholders of the same series of a class should be treated equally.
B.1.2	Where the company has more than one class of shares, does the company publicise the voting rights attached to each class of shares (e.g. through the company website/reports/ the stock exchange/the regulator's website)?	(1) Within any series of a class, all shares should carry the same rights. All investors should be able to obtain information about the rights attached to all series and classes of shares before they purchase. Any changes in voting rights should be subject to approval by those classes of shares which are negatively affected. ICGN 8.3.1 Unequal voting rights Companies ordinary or common shares should feature one vote for one share. Divergence from a 'one-share, one-vote' standard which gives certain shareholders power which is disproportionate to their equity ownership should be both disclosed and justified.

B.2	Notice of AGM	Guiding Reference
B.2.1	Does each resolution in the most recent AGM deal with only one item, i.e., there is no bundling of several items into the same resolution?	OECD Principle II: (C) Shareholders should have the opportunity to participate effectively and vote in general shareholder meetings and should be informed of the rules, including voting procedures, that govern shareholder meetings: Shareholders should be furnished with sufficient and timely information concerning the date, location and agenda of general meetings, as well as full and timely information regarding the issues to be decided at the meeting.
B.2.2	Are the company's notices of the most recent AGM/circulars fully translated into English and published on the same date as the local-language version?	Effective shareholder participation in key corporate governance decisions, such as the nomination and election of board members, should be facilitated.

B.2	Notice of AGM	Guiding Reference
Does the notice of AGM/circulars have the following details:		
B.2.3	Are the profiles of directors/commissioners (at least age, academic qualification, date of first appointment, experience, and directorships in other listed companies) in seeking election/re-election included?	**OECD Principle II:** (A) All shareholders of the same series of a class should be treat equally. (4) Impediments to cross border voting should be eliminated. **ICGN 8.3.2 Shareholder participation in governance** Shareholders should have the right to participate in key corporate governance decisions, such as the right to nominate, appoint and remove directors in an individual basis and also the right to appoint external auditor. **ICGN 8.4.1 Shareholder ownership rights** The exercise of ownership rights by all shareholders should be facilitated, including giving shareholders timely and adequate notice of all matters proposed for shareholder vote.
B.2.4	Are the auditors seeking appointment/re-appointment clearly identified?	
B.2.5	Has an explanation of the dividend policy been provided?	
B.2.6	Is the amount payable for final dividends disclosed?	
B.2.7	Were the proxy documents made easily available?	

B.3	Insider trading and abusive self-dealing should be prohibited.	Guiding Reference
B.3.1	Does the company have policies and/or rules prohibiting directors/commissioners and employees to benefit from knowledge which is not generally available to the market?	**OECD Principle III:** (B) Insider trading and abusive dealing should be prohibited **ICGN 3.5 Employee share dealing** Companies should have clear rules regarding any trading by directors and employees in the company's own securities. Among other issues, these must seek to ensure individuals do not benefit from knowledge which is not generally available to the market. **ICGN 8.5 Shareholder rights of action** ... Minority shareholders should be afforded protection and remedies against abusive or oppressive conduct.
B.3.2	Are the directors/commissioners required to report their dealings in company shares within 3 business days?	

B.4	Related party transactions by directors and key executives.	Guiding Reference
B.4.1	Does the company have a policy requiring directors/commissioners to disclose their interest in transactions and any other conflicts of interest?	**OECD Principle III:** (C) Members of the board and key executives should be required to disclose to the board whether they, directly, indirectly or on behalf of third parties, have a material interest in any transaction or matter directly affecting the corporation.
B.4.2	Does the company have a policy requiring a committee of independent directors/ commissioners to review material/significant RPTs to determine whether they are in the best interests of the company and shareholders?	**ICGN 2.11.1 Related party transactions** Companies should have a process for reviewing and monitoring any related party transaction. A committee of independent directors should review significant related party transactions to determine whether they are in the best interests of the company and if so to determine what terms are fair.
B.4.3	Does the company have a policy requiring board members (directors/commissioners) to abstain from participating in the board discussion on a particular agenda when they are conflicted?	**ICGN 2.11.2 Director conflicts of interest** Companies should have a process for identifying and managing conflicts of interest directors may have. If a director has an interest in a matter under consideration by the board, then the director should not participate in those discussions and the board should follow any further appropriate processes. Individual directors should be conscious of shareholder and public perceptions and seek to avoid situations where there might be an appearance of a conflict of interest.
B.4.4	Does the company have policies on loans to directors and commissioners either forbidding this practice or ensuring that they are being conducted at arm's length basis and at market rates?	

B.5	Protecting minority shareholders from abusive actions	Guiding Reference
B.5.1	Were there any RPTs that can be classified as financial assistance to entities other than wholly-owned subsidiary companies?	**OECD Principle III** (A) All shareholders of the same series of a class should be treated equally. (2) Minority shareholders should be protected from abusive actions by, or in the interest of, controlling shareholders acting either directly or indirectly, and should have effective means of redress. **ICGN 2.11.1 Related party transactions** Companies should have a process for reviewing and monitoring any related party transaction. A committee of independent directors should review significant related party transactions to determine whether they are in the best interests of the company and if so to determine what terms are fair.

B.5	Protecting minority shareholders from abusive actions	Guiding Reference
B.5.2	Does the company disclose that RPTs are conducted in such a way to ensure that they are fair and at arms' length?	**ICGN 2.11.2 Director conflicts of interest** Companies should have a process for identifying and managing conflicts of interest directors may have. If a director has an interest in a matter under consideration by the board, then the director should not participate in those discussions and the board should follow any further appropriate processes. Individual directors should be conscious of shareholder and public perceptions and seek to avoid situations where there might be an appearance of a conflict of interest. **ICGN 8.5 Shareholder rights of action** Shareholders should be afforded rights of action and remedies which are readily accessible in order to redress conduct of company which treats them inequitably. Minority shareholders should be afforded protection and remedies against abusive or oppressive conduct.
B.5.3	In case of related party transactions requiring shareholders' approval, is the decision made by disinterested shareholders?	**OECD Principles III. A (2):** Minority shareholders must be protected from abusive actions by, or in the interest of controlling shareholders acting either directly or indirectly, and should have effective means of redress.

C.   Role of Stakeholders

C.1	The rights of stakeholders that are established by law or through mutual agreements are to be respected.	Guiding Reference
Does the company disclose a policy that :		
C.1.1	Stipulates the existence and scope of the company's efforts to address customers' welfare?	**OECD Principle IV (A):** The rights of stakeholders that are established by law or through mutual agreements are to be respected. In all OECD countries, the rights of stakeholders are established by law (e.g. labour, business, commercial and insolvency laws) or by contractual relations. Even in areas where stakeholder interests are not legislated, many firms make additional commitments to stakeholders, and concern over corporate reputation and corporate performance often requires the recognition of broader interests.
C.1.2	Explains supplier/contractor selection practice?	
C.1.3	Describes the company's efforts to ensure that its value chain is environmentally friendly or is consistent with promoting sustainable development?	
C.1.4	Elaborates the company's efforts to interact with the communities in which they operate?	

C.1	The rights of stakeholders that are established by law or through mutual agreements are to be respected.	Guiding Reference
C.1.5	Describe the company's anti-corruption programmes and procedures?	Global Reporting Initiative: Sustainability Report (C1.1–C.15) International Accounting Standards 1: Presentation of Financial Statements
C.1.6	Describes how creditors' rights are safeguarded?	

Does the company disclose the activities that it has undertaken to implement the above mentioned policies?

C.1.7	Customer health and safety	OECD Principle IV (A) & Global Reporting Initiative
C.1.8	Supplier/Contractor selection and criteria	
C.1.9	Environmentally-friendly value chain	
C.1.10	Interaction with the communities	
C.1.11	Anti-corruption programmes and procedures	
C.1.12	Creditors' rights	
C.1.13	Does the company have a separate corporate responsibility (CR) report/section or sustainability report/section?	OECD Principle V (A): Disclosure should include, but not be limited to, material information on: (7) Issues regarding employees and other stakeholders. Companies are encouraged to provide information on key issues relevant to employees and other stakeholders that may materially affect the long term sustainability of the company.

C.2	Where stakeholder interests are protected by law, stakeholders should have the opportunity to obtain effective redress for violation of their rights.	Guiding Reference
C.2.1	Does the company provide contact details via the company's website or Annual Report which stakeholders (e.g. customers, suppliers, general public etc.) can use to voice their concerns and/or complaints for possible violation of their rights?	OECD Principle IV (B): Where stakeholder interests are protected by law, stakeholders should have the opportunity to obtain effective redress for violation of their rights. The governance framework and processes should be transparent and not impede the ability of stakeholders to communicate and to obtain redress for the violation of rights.

C.3	Performance-enhancing mechanisms for employee participation should be permitted to develop.	Guiding Reference
C.3.1	Does the company explicitly disclose the health, safety, and welfare policy for its employees?	**OECD Principle IV (C):** Performance-enhancing mechanisms for employee participation should be permitted to develop. In the context of corporate governance, performance enhancing mechanisms for participation may benefit companies directly as well as indirectly through the readiness by employees to invest in firm specific skills.
C.3.2	Does the company publish relevant information relating to health, safety and welfare of its employees?	
C.3.3	Does the company have training and development programmes for its employees?	Firm specific skills are those skills/competencies that are related to production technology and/or organizational aspects that are unique to a firm.
C.3.4	Does the company publish relevant information on training and development programmes for its employees?	Examples of mechanisms for employee participation include: employee representation on boards; and governance processes such as works councils that consider employee viewpoints in certain key decisions. With respect to performance enhancing mechanisms, employee stock ownership plans or other profit sharing mechanisms are to be found in many countries.
C.3.5	Does the company have a reward/compensation policy that accounts for the performance of the company beyond short-term financial measures?	

C.4	Stakeholders including individual employee and their representative bodies should be able to freely communicate their concerns about illegal or unethical practices to the board and their rights should not be compromised for doing this.	Guiding Reference
C.4.1	Does the company have procedures for complaints by employees concerning illegal (including corruption) and unethical behaviour?	**OECD Principle IV (E):** Stakeholders, including individual employees and their representative bodies, should be able to freely communicate their concerns about illegal or unethical practices to the board and their rights should not be compromised for doing this.
C.4.2	Does the company have a policy or procedures to protect an employee/person who reveals illegal/unethical behaviour from retaliation?	

D. Disclosure and Transparency

D.1	Transparent ownership structure	Guiding Reference
D.1.1	Does the information on shareholdings reveal the identity of beneficial owners, holding 5% shareholding or more?	**OECD Principle V: Disclosure and Transparency** (A) Disclosure should include, but not limited to, material information on: (3) Major share ownership and voting rights, including group structures, intra- group relations, ownership data, and beneficial ownership.
D.1.2	Does the company disclose the direct and indirect (deemed) shareholdings of major and/or substantial shareholders?	
D.1.3	Does the company disclose the direct and indirect (deemed) shareholdings of directors (commissioners)?	**ICGN 7.6 Disclosure of ownership** ... the disclosure should include a description of the relationship of the company to other companies in the corporate group, data on major shareholders and any other information necessary for a proper understanding of the company's relationship with its public shareholders.
D.1.4	Does the company disclose the direct and indirect (deemed) shareholdings of senior management?	
D.1.5	Does the company disclose details of the parent/holding company, subsidiaries, associates, joint ventures and special purpose enterprises/vehicles (SPEs)/(SPVs)?	

D.2	Quality of Annual Report	Guiding Reference
Does the company's annual report disclose the following items:		
D.2.1	Key risks	**OECD Principle V (A):** (1)The financial and operating results of the company; (2)Company objectives, including ethics, environment, and other public policy commitments; (3) Major share ownership and voting rights, including group structures, intra- group relations, ownership data, beneficial ownership; (4)Remuneration policy for members of the board and key executives, including their qualifications, the selection process, other company directorships and whether they are regarded as independent by the board; (5) Foreseeable risk factors, including risk management system; Issues regarding employees and other stakeholders; (6) Issues regarding employees and other stakeholders; (7) Governance structure and policies, in particular, the content of any corporate governance code or policy and the process by which it is implemented.
D.2.2	Corporate objectives	
D.2.3	Financial performance indicators	
D.2.4	Non-financial performance indicators	
D.2.5	Dividend policy	
D.2.6	Details of whistle-blowing policy	

D.2	Quality of Annual Report	Guiding Reference
D.2.7	Biographical details (at least age, qualifications, date of first appointment, relevant experience, and any other directorships of listed companies) of directors/commissioners	**OECD Principle V (E):** Channels for disseminating information should provide for equal, timely and cost-efficient access to relevant information by users.
D.2.8	Training and/or continuing education programme attended by each director/commissioner	**ICGN 2.4 Composition and structure of the board** **ICGN 2.4.1 Skills and experience** **ICGN 2.4.3 Independence**
D.2.9	Number of board of directors/commissioners meetings held during the year	**ICGN 5.0 Remuneration** **ICGN 5.4 Transparency**
D.2.10	Attendance details of each director/commissioner in respect of meetings held	**UK Corporate Governance Code (2010)** A.1.2 - the number of meetings of the board and those committees and individual attendance by directors.
D.2.11	Details of remuneration of each member of the board of directors/commissioners	**CLSA-ACGA (2010) CG Watch 2010 - Appendix 2** (I) CG rules and practices (19) Disclose the exact remuneration of individual directors.
D.2.12	Does the Annual Report contain a statement confirming the company's full compliance with the code of corporate governance and where there is non- compliance, identify and explain reasons for each such issue?	**OECD Principle V (A) (8):** **UK CODE (JUNE 2010): Listing Rules** 9.8.6 R (for UK incorporated companies) and 9.8.7 R (for overseas incorporated companies) state that in the case of a company that has a Premium listing of equity shares, the following items must be included in its Annual Report and accounts: a statement of how the listed company has applied the Main Principles set out in the UK CG Code, in a manner that would enable shareholders to evaluate how the principles have been applied; a statement as to whether the listed company has complied throughout the accounting period with all relevant provisions set out in the UK CG Code; or not complied throughout the accounting period with all relevant provisions set out in the UK CG Code, and if so, setting out: (i) those provisions, if any, it has not complied with; (ii) in the case of provisions whose requirements are of a continuing nature, the period within which, if any, it did not comply with some or all of those provisions; and (iii) the company's reasons for non-compliance.

D.2	Quality of Annual Report	Guiding Reference
		ASX CODE: Under ASX Listing Rule 4.10.3, companies are required to provide a statement in their Annual Report disclosing the extent to which they have followed the Recommendations in the reporting period. Where companies have not followed all the Recommendations, they must identify the Recommendations that have not been followed and give reasons for not following them. Annual Reporting does not diminish the company's obligation to provide disclosure under ASX Listing Rule 3.1.

D.3	Disclosure of related party transactions (RPT)	Guiding Reference
D.3.1	Does the company disclose its policy covering the review and approval of material/significant RPTs?	**OECD Principle V: Disclosure and Transparency:** (A) Disclosure should include, but not limited to, material information on: (5) Related party transactions
D.3.2	Does the company disclose the name of the related party and relationship for each material/significant RPT?	**ICGN 2.11.1 Related party transactions:** The company should disclose details of all material related party transactions in its Annual Report.
D.3.3	Does the company disclose the nature and value for each material/significant RPT?	

D.4	Directors and commissioners dealings in shares of the company	Guiding Reference
D.4.1	Does the company disclose trading in the company's shares by insiders?	**OECD Principle V (A):** (3) Major share ownership and voting rights **ICGN 3.5 Employee share dealing:** Companies should have clear rules regarding any trading by directors and employees in the company's own securities. **ICGN 5.5 Share ownership:** Every company should have and disclose a policy concerning ownership of shares of the company by senior managers and executive directors with the objective of aligning the interests of these key executives with those of shareholders.

D.5	External auditor and Auditor Report	Guiding Reference
D.5.1	Are audit fees disclosed? *Where the same audit firm is engaged for both audit and non-audit services?*	**OECD Principle V (C):** An annual audit should be conducted by an independent, competent and qualified, auditor in order to provide an external and objective assurance to the board and shareholders that the financial statements fairly represent the financial position and performance of the company in all material respects.
D.5.2	Are the non-audit fees disclosed?	**OECD Principle V (D):** External auditors should be accountable to the shareholders and owe a duty to the company to exercise due professional care in the conduct of the audit.
D.5.3	Does the non-audit fee exceed the audit fees?	**ICGN 6.5 Ethical standards (Audit):** The auditors should observe high-quality auditing and ethical standards. To limit the possible risk of possible conflicts of interest, non-audit services and fees paid to auditors for non-audit services should be both approved in advance by the audit committee and disclosed in the Annual Report.

D.6	Medium of communications	Guiding Reference
Does the company use the following modes of communication?		
D.6.1	Quarterly reporting	**OECD Principle V (E):** Channels for disseminating information should provide for equal, timely and cost-efficient access to relevant information by users.
D.6.2	Company website	
D.6.3	Analyst's briefing	**ICGN 7.1 Transparent and open communication:** Every company should aspire to transparent and open communication about its aims, its challenges, its achievements and its failures.
D.6.4	Media briefings/press conferences	**ICGN 7.2 Timely disclosure:** Companies should disclose relevant and material information concerning themselves on a timely basis, in particular meeting market guidelines where they exist, so as to allow investors to make informed decisions about the acquisition, ownership obligations and rights, and sales of shares.

D.7	Timely filing/release of annual/financial reports	Guiding Reference
D.7.1	Are the audited annual financial report/ statement released within 120 days from the financial year end?	**OECD Principle V (C)** **OECD Principle V (E)** **OECD Principle V (A):** **ICGN 7.2 Timely disclosure** **ICGN 7.3 Affirmation of financial statements** The board of directors and the corporate officers of the company should affirm at least annually the accuracy of the company's financial statements or financial accounts.
D.7.2	Is the annual report released within 120 days from the financial year end?	
D.7.3	Is the true and fairness/fair representation of the annual financial statement/reports affirmed by the board of directors/ commissioners and/or the relevant officers of the company?	

D.8	Company website	Guiding Reference
Does the company have a website disclosing up-to-date information on the following:		
D.8.1	Business operations	**OECD Principle V (A)** **OECD Principle V (E):** **ICGN 7.1 Transparent and open communication** **ICGN 7.2 Timely disclosure**
D.8.2	Financial statements/reports (current and prior years)	
D.8.3	Materials provided in briefings to analysts and media	
D.8.4	Shareholding structure	
D.8.5	Group corporate structure	
D.8.6	Downloadable annual report	
D.8.7	Notice of AGM and/or EGM	
D.8.8	Minutes of AGM and/or EGM	
D.8.9	Company's constitution (company's by-laws, memorandum and articles of association)	

D.9	Investor relations	Guiding Reference
D.9.1	Does the company disclose the contact details (e.g. telephone, fax, and email) of the officer/office responsible for investor relations?	**ICGN 7.1 Transparent and open communication**

E.   Responsibilities of the Board

E.1	Board Duties and Responsibilities	Guiding Reference
Clearly defined board responsibilities and corporate governance policy		
E.1.1	Does the company disclose its corporate governance policy/board charter?	**OECD Principle V: Disclosure and Transparency** (A) Disclosure should include, but not be limited to, material information on: (8) Governance structures and policies, in particular, the content of any corporate governance code or policy and the process by which it is implemented.
E.1.2	Are the types of decisions requiring board of directors/commissioners' approval disclosed?	**OECD Principle VI (D)**
E.1.3	Are the roles and responsibilities of the board of directors/commissioners clearly stated?	**OECD Principle VI: The Responsibilities of the Board** (D) The board should fulfil certain key functions, including: (1) Reviewing and guiding corporate strategy, major plans of action, risk policy, annual budgets and business plans; setting performance objectives; monitoring implementation and corporate performance; and overseeing major capital expenditures, acquisitions and divestitures. (2) Monitoring the effectiveness of the company's governance practices and making changes as needed. (3) Selecting, compensating, monitoring and, when necessary, replacing key executives and overseeing succession planning. (4) Aligning key executive and board remuneration with the longer term interests of the company and its shareholders. (5) Ensuring a formal and transparent board nomination and election process. (6) Monitoring and managing potential conflicts of interest of management, board members and shareholders, including misuse of corporate assets and abuse in related party transactions. (7) Ensuring the integrity of the corporation's accounting and financial reporting systems, including the independent audit, and that appropriate systems of control are in place, in particular, systems for risk management, financial and operational control, and compliance with the law and relevant standards. (8) Overseeing the process of disclosure and communications.

E.1	Board Duties and Responsibilities	Guiding Reference
Corporate Vision/Mission		
E.1.4	Does the company have a vision and mission statement?	**OECD Principle 6 (P58)** **ICGN:3.2 Integrity**
E.1.5	Has the board review the vision and mission/strategy in the last financial year?	
E.1.6	Does the board of directors monitor/ oversee the implementation of the corporate strategy?	**ICGN: 3.2 Integrity** The board is responsible for overseeing the implementation and maintenance of a culture of integrity. The board should encourage a culture of integrity permeating all aspects of the co., and secure that its vision, mission and objectives are ethically sound.

E.2	Board structure	Guiding Reference
Code of Ethics or Conduct		
E.2.1	Are the details of the code of ethics or conduct disclosed?	**OECD Principle VI:** (C) The board should apply high ethical standards. It should take into account the interests of stakeholders.
E.2.2	Does the company disclose that all directors/ commissioners, senior management and employees are required to comply with the code?	The board has a key role in setting the ethical tone of a company, not only by its own actions, but also in appointing and overseeing key executives and consequently the management in general. High ethical standards are in the long term interests of the company as a means to make it credible and trustworthy, not only in day-to-day operations but also with respect to longer term commitments.
E.2.3	Does the company disclose how it implements and monitors compliance with the code of ethics or conduct?	To make the objectives of the board clear and operational, many companies have found it useful to develop company codes of conduct based on, inter alia, professional standards and sometimes broader codes of behaviour. The latter might include a voluntary commitment by the company (including its subsidiaries) to comply with the OECD Guidelines for Multinational Enterprises which reflect all four principles contained in the ILO Declaration on Fundamental Labour Rights.

E.2	Board structure	Guiding Reference
		Company-wide codes serve as a standard for conduct by both the board and key executives, setting the framework for the exercise of judgement in dealing with varying and often conflicting constituencies. At a minimum, the ethical code should set clear limits on the pursuit of private interests, including dealings in the shares of the company. An overall framework for ethical conduct goes beyond compliance with the law, which should always be a fundamental requirement.
E.2.4	Do independent directors/commissioners make up at least 50% of the board of directors/commissioners?	**OECD Principle VI (E):** In order to exercise its duties of monitoring managerial performance, preventing conflicts of interest and balancing competing demands on the corporation, it is essential that the board is able to exercise objective judgement. In the first instance this will mean independence and objectivity with respect to management with important implications for the composition and structure of the board. Board independence in these circumstances usually requires that a sufficient number of board members will need to be independent of management. The ASX Code recommends at least a majority of independent directors, while the UK Code recommends at least half of the board, excluding the Chairman, be independent directors. The minimum of three independent directors is to ensure that companies with small boards have enough independent directors (note that stock exchange rules often require at least two independent directors).
E.2.5	Are the independent directors/commissioners independent of management and major/substantial shareholders?	**OECD Principle VI (E):** In order to exercise its duties of monitoring managerial performance, preventing conflicts of interest and balancing competing demands on the corporation, it is essential that the board is able to exercise objective judgement. In the first instance this will mean independence and objectivity with respect to management with important implications for the composition and structure of the board. Board independence in these circumstances usually requires that a sufficient number of board members will need to be independent of management.

E.2	Board structure	Guiding Reference
		The variety of board structures, ownership patterns and practices in different countries will thus require different approaches to the issue of board objectivity. In many instances objectivity requires that a sufficient number of board members not be employed by the company or its affiliates and not be closely related to the company or its management through significant economic, family or other ties. This does not prevent shareholders from being board members. In others, independence from controlling shareholders or another controlling body will need to be emphasised, in particular if the *ex- ante* rights of minority shareholders are weak and opportunities to obtain redress are limited. This has led to both codes, and the law in some jurisdictions, to call for some board members to be independent of dominant shareholders, independence extending to not being their representative or having close business ties with them.
E.2.6	Does the company have a term limit of nine years or less for its independent directors/commissioners?	**UK CODE (JUNE 2010):** Non-executive directors should be appointed for specified terms subject to re- election and to statutory provisions relating to the removal of a director. Any term beyond six years for a non-executive director should be subject to particularly rigorous review, and should take into account the need for progressive refreshing of the board and to succession for appointments to the board and to senior management, so as to maintain an appropriate balance of skills and experience within the company and on the board.
E.2.7	Has the company set a limit of five board seats that an individual independent/non-executive director/commissioner may hold simultaneously?	**OECD Principle VI (E):** (3) Board members should be able to commit themselves effectively to their responsibilities. Service on too many boards can interfere with the performance of board members. Companies may wish to consider whether multiple board memberships by the same person are compatible with effective board performance and disclose the information to shareholders.
E.2.8	Does the company have any executive directors who serve on more than two boards of listed companies outside of the group?	

E.2	Board structure	Guiding Reference
Nominating Committee		
E.2.9	Does the company have a Nominating Committee (NC)?	**OECD Principle II (C):** (3) Effective shareholder participation in key corporate governance decisions, such as the nomination and election of board members, should be facilitated. Shareholders should be able to make their views known on the remuneration policy for board members and key executives. The equity component of compensation schemes for board members and employees should be subject to shareholder approval.
E.2.10	Does the Nominating Committee comprise of a majority of independent directors/commissioners?	With respect to nomination of candidates, boards in many companies have established Nominating Committees to ensure proper compliance with established nomination procedures and to facilitate and coordinate the search for a balanced and qualified board. It is increasingly regarded as good practice in many countries for independent board members to have a key role on this committee. To further improve the selection process, the Principles also call for full disclosure of the experience and background of candidates for the board and the nomination process, which will allow an informed assessment of the abilities and suitability of each candidate. **OECD Principle VI (E):** (1) Boards should consider assigning a sufficient number of non-executive board members capable of exercising independent judgement to tasks where there is a potential for conflict of interest. Examples of such key responsibilities are ensuring the integrity of financial and non-financial reporting, the review of related party transactions, nomination of board members and key executives, and board remuneration.
E.2.11	Is the chairman of the Nominating Committee an independent director/commissioner?	This item is in most codes of corporate governance.

E.2	Board structure	Guiding Reference
E.2.12	Does the company disclose the terms of reference/governance structure/charter of the Nominating Committee?	**OECD Principle VI (E):** (2) When committees of the board are established, their mandate, composition and working procedures should be well defined and disclosed by the board.
E.2.13	Did the Nominating Committee meet at least twice during the year?	While the use of committees may improve the work of the board they may
E.2.14	Is the attendance of members at Nominating Committee meetings disclosed?	also raise questions about the collective responsibility of the board and of individual board members. In order to evaluate the merits of board committees it is therefore important that the market receives a full and clear picture of their purpose, duties and composition. Such information is particularly important in an increasing number of jurisdictions where boards are establishing independent Audit Committees with powers to oversee the relationship with the external auditor and to act in many cases independently. Other such committees include those dealing with nomination and compensation. The accountability of the rest of the board and the board as a whole should be clear. Disclosure should not extend to committees set up to deal with, for example, confidential commercial transactions
		Given the responsibilities of the NC spelt out in codes of corporate governance, the NC is unlikely to be fulfilling these responsibilities effectively if it is only meeting once a year. Globally, the NC of large companies would meet several times a year.
Remuneration Committee/Compensation Committee		
E.2.15	Does the company have a Remuneration Committee?	**OECD Principle VI (D):** (4) Aligning key executive and board remuneration with the longer term interests of the company and its shareholders.
E.2.16	Does the Remuneration Committee comprise of a majority of independent directors/commissioners?	It is considered good practice in an increasing number of countries that remuneration policy and employment contracts for board members and key executives be handled
E.2.17	Is the chairman of the Remuneration Committee an independent director/commissioner?	by a special committee of the board comprising either wholly or a majority of independent directors. There are also calls for a Remuneration Committee that excludes executives that serve on each other's' Remuneration Committees, which could lead to conflicts of interest.

E.2	Board structure	Guiding Reference
E.2.18	Does the company disclose the terms of reference/governance structure/charter of the Remuneration Committee?	**OECD Principle VI (E):** (2) When committees of the board are established, their mandate, composition and working procedures should be well defined and disclosed by the board.
E.2.19	Did the Remuneration Committee meet at least twice during the year?	While the use of committees may improve the work of the board they may
E.2.20	Is the attendance of members at Remuneration Committee meetings disclosed?	also raise questions about the collective responsibility of the board and of individual board members. In order to evaluate the merits of board committees it is therefore important that the market receives a full and clear picture of their purpose, duties and composition. Such information is particularly important in an increasing number of jurisdictions where boards are establishing independent Audit Committees with powers to oversee the relationship with the external auditor and to act in many cases independently. Other such committees include those dealing with nomination and compensation. The accountability of the rest of the board and the board as a whole should be clear. Disclosure should not extend to committees set up to deal with, for example, confidential commercial transactions
		Given the responsibilities of the Remuneration Committee (RC) which are spelt out in codes of corporate governance, the RC is unlikely to be fulfilling these responsibilities effectively if it only meets once a year. Globally, the RC of large companies would meet several times a year.
Audit Committee		
E.2.21	Does the company have an Audit Committee?	**OECD Principle VI (E):** (1) Boards should consider assigning a sufficient number of non-executive board members capable of exercising independent judgement to tasks where there is a potential for conflict of interest. Examples of such key responsibilities are ensuring the integrity of financial and non-financial reporting, the review of related party transactions, nomination of board members and key executives, and board remuneration.

E.2	Board structure	Guiding Reference
E.2.22	Does the Audit Committee comprise entirely of non-executive directors/commissioners with a majority of independent directors/ commissioners?	**OECD Principle VI (E):** (2) When committees of the board are established, their mandate, composition and working procedures should be well defined and disclosed by the board.
E.2.23	Is the chairman of the Audit Committee an independent director/commissioner?	While the use of committees may improve the work of the board they may also raise questions about the collective responsibility of the board and of
E.2.24	Does the company disclose the terms of reference/governance structure/charter of the Audit Committee?	individual board members. In order to evaluate the merits of board committees it is therefore important that the market receives a full and clear picture of their purpose, duties and composition. Such information is particularly important in the increasing number of jurisdictions where boards are establishing independent Audit Committees with powers to oversee the relationship with the external auditor and to act in many cases independently. Other such committees include those dealing with nomination and compensation. The accountability of the rest of the board and the board as a whole should be clear. Disclosure should not extend to committees set up to deal with, for example, confidential commercial transactions.
E.2.25	Does the Annual Report disclose the profile or qualifications of the Audit Committee members?	Most codes specify the need for accounting/finance expertise or experience.
E.2.26	Does at least one of the independent directors/commissioners of the committee have accounting expertise (accounting qualification or experience)?	**UK CODE (JUNE 2010)** C.3.1. The board should satisfy itself that at least one member of the Audit Committee has recent and relevant financial experience.
E.2.27	Did the Audit Committee meet at least four times during the year?	As many of the key responsibilities of the Audit Committee are accounting- related, such as oversight of financial reporting and audits, it is important to have someone specifically with accounting expertise, not just general financial expertise.
E.2.28	Is the attendance of members at Audit Committee meetings disclosed?	

E.2	Board structure	Guiding Reference
E.2.29	Does the Audit Committee have primary responsibility for recommendation on the appointment, and removal of the external auditor?	**UK CODE (JUNE 2010)** C.3.6 The Audit Committee should have primary responsibility for making a recommendation on the appointment, reappointment and removal of the external auditor. If the board does not accept the Audit Committee's recommendation, it should include in the Annual Report, and in any papers recommending appointment or re-appointment, a statement from the Audit Committee explaining the recommendation and should set out reasons why the board has taken a different position.

E.3	Board Processes	Guiding Reference
Board meetings and attendance		
E.3.1	Are the board of directors meeting scheduled before the start of financial year?	Scheduling board meetings before or at the beginning of the year would allow directors to plan ahead to attend such meetings, thereby helping to maximise participation, especially as non-executive directors often have other commitments. Additional ad hoc meetings can always be scheduled if and when necessary. It is common practice for boards in developed markets to schedule meetings in this way.
E.3.2	Does the board of directors/commissioners meet at least six times during the year?	**WORLD BANK PRINCIPLE 6** (VI.I.24) Does the board meet at least six times per year? **INDO SCORECARD** E.10. How many meetings were held in the past year? If the board met more than six times, the firm earns a 'Y' score. If four to six meetings, the firm was scored as 'fair', while less than four times was scored as 'N'.
E.3.3	Has each of the directors/commissioners attended at least 75% of all the board meetings held during the year?	**OECD Principle VI (E):** (3) Board members should be able to commit themselves effectively to their responsibilities. Specific limitations may be less important than ensuring that members of the board enjoy legitimacy and confidence in the eyes of shareholders. Achieving legitimacy would also be facilitated by the publication of attendance records for individual board members (e.g. whether they have missed a significant number of meetings) and any other work undertaken on behalf of the board and the associated remuneration.

E.3	Board Processes	Guiding Reference
E.3.4	Does the company require a minimum quorum of at least 2/3 for board decisions?	**WORLD BANK PRINCIPLE 6** (VI.I.28) Is there a minimum quorum of at least 2/3 for board decisions to be valid?
E.3.5	Did the non-executive directors/commissioners of the company meet separately at least once during the year without any executives present?	**WORLD BANK PRINCIPLE 6** (VI.E.1.6) Does the corporate governance framework requires or encourages boards to conduct executive sessions?
Access to information		
E.3.6	Are board papers for board of directors/commissioners meetings provided to the board at least five business days in advance of the board meeting?	**OECD Principle VI:** (F) In order to fulfil their responsibilities, board members should have access to accurate, relevant and timely information. Board members require relevant information on a timely basis in order to support their decision-making. Non-executive board members do not typically have the same access to information as key managers within the company. The contributions of non-executive board members to the company can be enhanced by providing access to certain key managers within the company such as, for example, the company secretary and the internal auditor, and recourse to independent external advice at the expense of the company. In order to fulfil their responsibilities, board members should ensure that they obtain accurate, relevant and timely information. **WORLD BANK PRINCIPLE 6** (VI.F.2) Does such information need to be provided to the board at least five business days in advance of the board meeting?
E.3.7	Does the company secretary play a significant role in supporting the board in discharging its responsibilities?	**OECD Principle VI (F):** **ICSA Guidance on the Corporate Governance Role of the Company Secretary**
E.3.8	Is the company secretary trained in legal, accountancy or company secretarial practices?	**WORLD BANK PRINCIPLE 6** (VI.D.2.12) Do company boards have a professional and qualified company secretary?

E.3	Board Processes	Guiding Reference
Board Appointments and Re-Election		
E.3.9	Does the company disclose the criteria used in selecting new directors/commissioners?	**OECD Principle II (C) (3):** To further improve the selection process, the Principles also call for full disclosure of the experience and background of candidates for the board and the nomination process, which will allow an informed assessment of the abilities and suitability of each candidate.
E.3.10	Does the company disclose the process followed in appointing new directors/commissioners?	**OECD Principle VI (D):** (5) Ensuring a formal and transparent board nomination and election process. These Principles promote an active role for shareholders in the nomination and election of board members. The board has an essential role to play in ensuring that this and other aspects of the nominations and election process are respected. First, while actual procedures for nomination may differ among countries, the board or a nomination committee has a special responsibility to make sure that established procedures are transparent and respected. Second, the board has a key role in identifying potential members for the board with the appropriate knowledge, competencies and expertise to complement the existing skills of the board and thereby improve its value- adding potential for the company. In several countries there are calls for an open search process extending to a broad range of people.
E.3.11	Are all the directors/commissioners subject to re-election at least once every three years?	**ICGN: 2.9.1** Election of directors: Directors should be conscious of their accountability to shareholders, and many jurisdictions have mechanisms to ensure that this is in place on an on-going basis. There are some markets however where such accountability is less apparent and in these each director should stand for election on an annual basis. Elsewhere directors should stand for election at least once every three years, though they should face evaluation more frequently.
		WORLD BANK PRINCIPLE 6 (VI.I.18) Can the re-election of board members be staggered over time? (Staggered boards are those where only a part of the board is re-elected at each election, e.g. only 1/3 of directors are re-elected every year.)

E.3	Board Processes	Guiding Reference
Remuneration Matters		
E.3.12	Does the company disclose its remuneration (fees, allowances, benefit-in-kind and other emoluments) policy/practices (i.e. the use of short term and long term incentives and performance measures) for its executive directors and CEO?	**OECD Principle VI (D):** (4) Aligning key executive and board remuneration with the longer term interests of the company and its shareholders. In an increasing number of countries it is regarded as good practice for boards to develop and disclose a remuneration policy statement covering board members and key executives. Such policy statements specify the relationship between remuneration and performance, and include measurable standards that emphasise the longer run interests of the company over short term considerations. Policy statements generally tend to set conditions for payments to board members for extra-board activities, such as consulting. They also often specify terms to be observed by board members and key executives about holding and trading the stock of the company, and the procedures to be followed in granting and re-pricing of options. In some countries, policy also covers the payments to be made when terminating the contract of an executive.
E.3.13	Is there disclosure of the fee structure for non-executive directors/commissioners?	**UK CODE (JUNE 2010)** D.1.3 Levels of remuneration for non-executive directors should reflect the time commitment and responsibilities of the role. Disclosure of fee structure for non-executive directors allows shareholders to assess if these directors are remunerated in an appropriate manner, for example, whether they are paid for taking on additional responsibilities and contributions, such as chairing committees.
E.3.14	Do the shareholders or the Board of Directors approve the remuneration of the executive directors and/or the senior executives?	**OECD Principle VI. (D.4):** The Board should fulfil certain key functions including aligning key executive and board remuneration with the longer term interests of the company and its shareholders. **ICGN 2.3 (D) and (E)** D. Selecting, remunerating, monitoring and where necessary replacing key executives and overseeing succession planning. E. Aligning key executives and Board remuneration with the longer term interest of the company and its shareholders.

E.3	Board Processes	Guiding Reference
E.3.15	Do independent non-executive directors/commissioners receive options, performance shares or bonuses?	**UK CODE (JUNE 2010)** (D.1.3) Levels of remuneration for non-executive directors should reflect the time commitment and responsibilities of the role. Remuneration for non- executive directors should not include share options or other performance- related elements. If, by exception, options are granted, shareholder approval should be sought in advance and any shares acquired by exercise of the options should be held until at least one year after the non-executive director leaves the board. Holding of share options could be relevant to the determination of a non-executive director's independence (as set out in provision B.1.1). **ASX CODE** Box 8.2: Guidelines for non-executive director remuneration Companies may find it useful to consider the following when considering non-executive director remuneration: (1) Non-executive directors should normally be remunerated by way of fees, in the form of cash, noncash benefits, superannuation contributions or salary sacrifice into equity; they should not normally participate in schemes designed for the remuneration of executives. (2) Non-executive directors should not receive options or bonus payments. (3) Non-executive directors should not be provided with retirement benefits other than superannuation.
Internal Audit		
E.3.16	Does the company have a separate internal audit function?	**OECD Principle VI (D)** (7) Ensuring the integrity of the corporation's accounting and financial reporting systems, including the independent audit, and that appropriate systems of control are in place, in particular, systems for risk management, financial and operational control, and compliance with the law and relevant standards. Ensuring the integrity of the essential reporting and monitoring systems will require the board to set and enforce clear lines of responsibility and accountability throughout the organisation. The board will also need to ensure that there is appropriate oversight by senior management. One way of doing this is through an internal audit system directly reporting to the board.

E.3	Board Processes	Guiding Reference
E.3.17	Is the head of internal audit identified or, if outsourced, is the name of the external firm disclosed?	Companies often disclose that they have an internal audit but, in practice, it is not uncommon for it to exist more in form than in substance. For example, the in-house internal audit may be assigned to someone with other operational responsibilities. As internal audit is unregulated, unlike external audit, there are firms providing outsourced internal audit services which are not properly qualified to do so. Making the identity of the head of internal audit or the external service provider public would provide some level of safeguard that the internal audit is substantive.
E.3.18	Does the appointment and removal of the internal auditor require the approval of the Audit Committee?	**OECD Principle VI (D) (7):** In some jurisdictions it is considered good practice for the internal auditors to report to an independent Audit Committee of the board or an equivalent body which is also responsible for managing the relationship with the external auditor, thereby allowing a coordinated response by the board. **WORLD BANK PRINCIPLE 6** (VI.D.7.9) Does the internal auditors have direct and unfettered access to the board of directors and its independent Audit Committee? **ASX Principles on CG** "...companies should consider a second reporting line from the internal audit function to the board or relevant committee." Under the ASX Principles it is also recommended that the Audit Committee have access to internal audit without the presence of management, and that "the audit committee should recommend to the board the appointment and dismissal of a chief internal audit executive."
Risk Oversight		
E.3.19	Does the company disclose the internal control procedures/risk management systems it has in place?	**OECD Principle 6 (VI) (D) (7):** Ensuring the integrity of the corporation's accounting and financial reporting systems, including the independent audit, and that appropriate systems of control are in place, in particular, systems for risk management, financial and operational control, and compliance with the law and relevant standards.

E.3	Board Processes	Guiding Reference
E.3.20	Does the Annual Report disclose that the board of directors/commissioners has conducted a review of the company's material controls (including operational, financial and compliance controls) and risk management systems?	**UK CODE (JUNE 2010)** C.2.1 The board should, at least annually, conduct a review of the effectiveness of the company's risk management and internal control systems and should report to shareholders that they have done so. The review should cover all material controls, including financial, operational and compliance controls.
E.3.21	Does the company disclose how key risks are managed?	**OECD Principle V (A):** (6) Foreseeable risk factors. Disclosure of risk is most effective when it is tailored to the particular industry in question. Disclosure about the system for monitoring and managing risk is increasingly regarded as good practice.
E.3.22	Does the Annual Report contain a statement from the board of directors/commissioners or Audit Committee commenting on the adequacy of the company's Internal controls/risk management systems?	**OECD Principle 6 (VI) (D):** (7) Ensuring the integrity of the corporation's accounting and financial reporting systems, including the independent audit, and that appropriate systems of control are in place, in particular, systems for risk management, financial and operational control, and compliance with the law and relevant standards. In some jurisdictions it is considered good practice for the internal auditors to report to an independent audit committee of the board or an equivalent body which is also responsible for managing the relationship with the external auditor, thereby allowing a coordinated response by the board. It should also be regarded as good practice for this committee, or equivalent body, to review and report to the board the most critical accounting policies which are the basis for financial reports. However, the board should retain final responsibility for ensuring the integrity of the reporting systems. Some countries have provided for the chair of the board to report on the internal control process.

E.3	Board Processes	Guiding Reference
E.3.22	Does the Annual Report contain a statement from the board of directors/commissioners or Audit Committee commenting on the adequacy of the company's internal controls/risk management systems?	**OECD Principle 6 (VI) (D):** (7) Ensuring the integrity of the corporation's accounting and financial reporting systems, including the independent audit, and that appropriate systems of control are in place, in particular, systems for risk management, financial and operational control, and compliance with the law and relevant standards. In some jurisdictions it is considered good practice for the internal auditors to report to an independent audit committee of the board or an equivalent body which is also responsible for managing the relationship with the external auditor, thereby allowing a coordinated response by the board. It should also be regarded as good practice for this committee, or equivalent body, to review and report to the board the most critical accounting policies which are the basis for financial reports. However, the board should retain final responsibility for ensuring the integrity of the reporting systems. Some countries have provided for the chair of the board to report on the internal control process.

E.4	People on the Board	Guiding Reference
Board Chairman		
E.4.1	Do different persons assume the roles of chairman and CEO?	**OECD Principle VI:** (E) The board should be able to exercise objective independent judgement on corporate affairs.
E.4.2	Is the chairman an independent director/commissioner?	In a number of countries with single tier board systems, the objectivity of the board and its independence from management may be strengthened by the separation of the role of chief executive and chairman, or, if these roles are combined, by designating a lead non-executive director to convene or chair sessions of the outside directors. Separation of the two posts may be regarded as good practice, as it can help to achieve an appropriate balance of power, increase accountability and improve the board's capacity for decision making independent of management.

E.4	People on the Board	Guiding Reference
E.4.3	Are any of the directors a former CEO of the company in the past 2 years?	**UK Code (June 2010)** A.3.1 The chairman should on appointment meet the independence criteria set out in B.1.1 below. A chief executive should not go on to be chairman of the same company. If, exceptionally, a board decides that a chief executive should become chairman, the board should consult major shareholders in advance and should set out its reasons to shareholders at the time of the appointment and in the next Annual Report. **ASX Code** Recommendation 3.2 The chief executive officer should not go on to become chair of the same company. A former chief executive officer will not qualify as an "independent" director unless there has been a period of at least three years between ceasing employment with the company and serving on the board.
E.4.4	Are the role and responsibilities of the chairman disclosed?	**ICGN: 2.5 Role of the Chair** The chair has the crucial function of setting the right context in terms of board agenda, the provision of information to directors, and open boardroom discussions, to enable the directors to generate the effective board debate and discussion and to provide the constructive challenge which the company needs. The chair should work to create and maintain the culture of openness and constructive challenge which allows a diversity of views to be expressed... The chair should be available to shareholders for dialogue on key matters of the company's governance and where shareholders have particular concerns.
Skills and Competencies		
E.4.5	Does at least one non-executive director/commissioner have prior working experience in the major sector that the company is operating in?	**ICGN: 2.4.3 Independence** Alongside appropriate skill, competence and experience, and the appropriate context to encourage effective behaviours, one of the principal features of a well-governed corporation is the exercise by its board of directors of independent judgement, meaning judgement in the best interests of the corporation, free of any external influence on any individual director, or the board as a whole. In order to provide this independent judgement, and to generate confidence that

E.4	People on the Board	Guiding Reference
		independent judgement is being applied, a board should include a strong presence of independent non-executive directors with appropriate competencies including key industry sector knowledge and experience. There should be at least a majority of independent directors on each board.
E.4.6	Does the company disclose a board of directors/commissioners diversity policy?	**ASX Code** Recommendation 3.2 Companies should establish a policy concerning diversity and disclose the policy or a summary of that policy. The policy should include requirements for the board to establish measurable objectives for achieving gender diversity and for the board to assess annually both the objectives and progress in achieving them. Regulations and codes of corporate governance in many developed markets now incorporate board diversity as a consideration in board composition.

E.5	Board Performance	Guiding Reference
Directors Development		
E.5.1	Does the company have orientation programmes for new directors/commissioners?	This item is in most codes of corporate governance.
E.5.2	Does the company have a policy that encourages directors/commissioners to attend on-going or continuous professional education programmes?	**OECD Principle VI (E):** (3) Board members should be able to commit themselves effectively to their responsibilities. In order to improve board practices and the performance of its members, an increasing number of jurisdictions are now encouraging companies to engage in board training and voluntary self-evaluation that meets the needs of the individual company. This might include that board members acquire appropriate skills upon appointment, and thereafter remain abreast of relevant new laws, regulations, and changing commercial risks through in-house training and external courses.

E.5	Board Performance	Guiding Reference
CEO/Executive Management Appointments and Performance		
E.5.3	Does the company disclose how the board of directors/commissioners plans for the succession of the CEO/Managing Director/President and key management?	**OECD Principle VI (D):** (3) Selecting, compensating, monitoring and, when necessary, replacing key executives and overseeing succession planning. In two tier board systems the supervisory board is also responsible for appointing the management board which will normally comprise most of the key executives.
E.5.4	Does the board of directors/commissioners conduct an annual performance assessment of the CEO/Managing Director/President?	**OECD Principle VI (D):** (2) Monitoring the effectiveness of the company's governance practices and making changes as needed. Monitoring of governance by the board also includes continuous review of the internal structure of the company to ensure that there are clear lines of accountability for management throughout the organisation. In addition to requiring the monitoring and disclosure of corporate governance practices on a regular basis, a number of countries have moved to recommend or indeed mandate self-assessment by boards of their performance as well as performance reviews of individual board members and the CEO/Chairman.
Board Appraisal		
E.5.5	Is an annual performance assessment conducted of the board of directors/commissioners?	**OECD Principle VI (D) (2)**
E.5.6	Does the company disclose the process followed in conducting the board assessment?	
E.5.7	Does the company disclose the criteria used in the board assessment?	
Director Appraisal		
E.5.8	Is an annual performance assessment conducted of individual director/commissioner?	**OECD Principle VI (D) (2)**
E.5.9	Does the company disclose the process followed in conducting the director/commissioner assessment?	
E.5.10	Does the company disclose the criteria used in the director/commissioner assessment?	

E.5	Board Performance	Guiding Reference
Committee Appraisal		
E.5.11	Is an annual performance assessment conducted of the board of directors/ commissioners committees?	**UK CODE (JUNE 2010)** B.6 Evaluation: The board should undertake a formal and rigorous annual evaluation of its own performance and that of its committees and individual directors.

LEVEL 2

BONUS
A. Rights of shareholders

A.1	Right to participate effectively in and vote in general shareholders meeting and should be informed of the rules, including voting procedures that govern general shareholders meeting.	Guiding Reference
A.1.1(B)	Does the company allow the use of secure electronic voting in absentia at the general meetings of shareholders?	**OECD Principle II (C):** (4) Shareholders should be able to vote in person or in absentia, and equal effect should be given to votes whether cast in person or in absentia.

B. Equitable treatment of shareholders

B.1	Notice of AGM	Guiding Reference
B.1.1(B)	Does the company release its notice of AGM (with detailed agendas and explanatory circulars), as announced to the Exchange, at least 28 days before the date of the meeting?	**OECD Principle II (C):** (1) Shareholders should be furnished with sufficient and timely information concerning the date, location and agenda of general meetings, as well as full and timely information regarding the issues to be decided at the meeting. (3) Effective shareholder participation in key corporate governance decisions, such as the nomination and election of board members, should be facilitated. **OECD Principle III (A):** **ICGN 8.3.2 Shareholder participation in governance** Shareholders should have the right to participate in key corporate governance decisions, such as the right to nominate, appoint and remove directors on an individual basis and also the right to appoint external auditors.

B.1	Notice of AGM	Guiding Reference
		ICGN 8.4.1 Shareholder ownership rights The exercise of ownership rights by all shareholders should be facilitated, including giving shareholders timely and adequate notice of all matters proposed for shareholder vote. **CLSA-ACGA (2010) CG Watch 2010 – Appendix 2.** (I) CG rules and practices (25) Do company release their AGM notices (with detailed agendas and explanatory circulars) at least 28 days before the date of the meeting?

C.   Roles of Stakeholders

C.1	The rights of stakeholders that are established by law or through mutual agreements are to be respected	Guiding Reference
C.1.1(B)	Does the company practice integrated report on its annual reports?	**International <IR> Framework – DRAFT IIRC Council Item 3b Meeting of 5 December 2013** "Integrated Reporting <IR> promotes a more cohesive and efficient approach to corporate reporting and aims to improve the quality of information available to providers of financial capital to enable a more efficient and productive allocation of capital. The IIRC's vision is a world in which integrated thinking is embedded within mainstream business practice in the public and private sectors, facilitated by <IR> as the corporate reporting norm."

D.   Disclosure and Transparency

D.1	Quality of Annual Report	Guiding Reference
D.1.1(B)	Are the audited annual Financial report/statement released within 60 days from the financial year end?	**OECD Principle V (C)** **OECD Principle V (E)** **ICGN 7.2 Timely disclosure** **ICGN 7.3 Affirmation of financial statements** The board of directors and the corporate officers of the company should affirm at least annually the accuracy of the company's financial statements or financial accounts.
D.1.2(B)	Does the company disclose details of remuneration of the CEO?	

E.   Responsibilities of the Board

E.1	Board Competencies and Diversity	Guiding Reference
E.1.1(B)	Does the company have at least one female independent director/commissioner?	**ICGN 2.4.1 Skills and experience** The board should consist of directors with the requisite range of skills, competence, knowledge, experience and approach, as well as a diversity of perspectives, to set the context for appropriate board behaviours and to enable it to discharge its duties and responsibilities effectively.

E.2	Nominating Committee	Guiding Reference
E.2.1(B)	Does the Nominating Committee comprise entirely of independent directors/commissioners?	**ICGN 2.4.4 Composition of board committees** The members of these key board committees should be solely non-executive directors, and in the case of the audit and remuneration committees, solely independent directors. All members of the nominations committee should be independent from management and at least a majority should be independent from dominant owners.
E.2.2(B)	Does the Nominating Committee undertake the process of identifying the quality of directors aligned with the company's strategic directions?	

E.3	Board Appointments and Re-Election	Guiding Reference
E.3.1(B)	Does the company use professional search firms or other external sources of candidates (such as director databases set up by director or shareholder bodies) when searching for candidates to the board of directors/commissioners?	**WORLD BANK PRINCIPLE 6** (VI.I.21) Are boards known to hire professional search firms when proposing candidates to the board?

E.4	Board Structure & Composition	Guiding Reference
E.4.1(B)	Do independent non-executive directors/commissioners make up more than 50% of the board of directors/commissioners?	

E.5	Board Performance	Guiding Reference
E.5.1(B)	Does the company have a separate level Risk Committee?	International Financial Corporation's Global Corporate Governance Forum Publication: When Do Companies Need a Board-level Risk Management Committee?(Volume 31, pp.11, March 2013)

E.5	Board Performance	Guiding Reference
		Benefits of a Board Level Risk Committee: (1) elevate risk oversight to the highest level in the company; (2) strengthen the quality of risk management; (3) inculcate a risk culture and risk-management environment to mitigate and manage risks effectively across the organization; (4) establish a platform for continuous assessment of risks in light of the changing internal and external environments; (5) improve communication among the board, management, and other stakeholders about risk management; and (6) demonstrate to internal and external stakeholders the company's commitment to risk management

PENALTY

A. Rights of shareholders

A.1	Basic shareholder rights	Guiding Reference
A.1.1(P)	Did the company fail or neglect to offer equal treatment for share repurchases to all shareholders?	**OECD Principle II (A)**

A.2	Shareholders, including institutional shareholders, should be allowed to consult with each other on issues concerning their basic shareholder rights as defined in the Principles, subject to exceptions to prevent abuse.	Guiding Reference
A.2.1(P):	Is there evidence of barriers that prevent shareholders from communicating or consulting with other shareholders?	**OECD Principle II (G):** Shareholders, including institutional shareholders, should be allowed to consult with each other on issues concerning their basic shareholder rights as defined in the Principles, subject to exceptions to prevent abuse.

A.3	Right to participate effectively in and vote in general shareholders meeting and should be informed of the rules, including voting procedures that govern general shareholders meeting.	Guiding Reference
A.3.1(P)	Did the company include any additional and unannounced agenda item into the notice of AGM/EGM?	**OECD Principle II (C) 2**

A.4	Capital structures and arrangements that enable certain shareholders to obtain a degree of control disproportionate to their equity ownership should be disclosed.	Guiding Reference
Did the company fail to disclose the existence of:		
A.4.1(P)	Shareholders agreement?	OECD Principle II (D)
A.4.2(P)	Voting cap?	
A.4.3(P)	Multiple voting rights?	

A.5	Capital structures and arrangements that enable certain shareholders to obtain a degree of control disproportionate to their equity ownership should be disclosed.	Guiding Reference
A.5.1(P)	Is a pyramid ownership structure and/or cross holding structure apparent?	OECD Principle II (D): Capital structures and arrangements that enable certain shareholders to obtain a degree of control disproportionate to their equity ownership should be disclosed. Some capital structures allow a shareholder to exercise a degree of control over the corporation disproportionate to the shareholders' equity ownership in the company. Pyramid structures, cross shareholdings and shares with limited or multiple voting rights can be used to diminish the capability of non-controlling shareholders to influence corporate policy.

B.   Equitable treatment of shareholders

B.1	Insider trading and abusive self-dealing should be prohibited.	Guiding Reference
B.1.1(P)	Has there been any conviction of insider trading involving directors/commissioners, management and employees in the past three years?	**OECD Principle III: The Equitable Treatment of Shareholders** (B) Insider trading and abusive dealing should be prohibited. **ICGN 3.5 Employee share dealing** Companies should have clear rules regarding any trading by directors and employees in the company's own securities. Among other issues, these must seek to ensure individuals do not benefit from knowledge which is not generally available to the market. **ICGN 8.5 Shareholder rights of action** ... Minority shareholders should be afforded protection and remedies against abusive or oppressive conduct.

B.2	Protecting minority shareholders from abusive action	Guiding Reference
B.2.1(P)	Has there been any cases of noncompliance with the laws, rules and regulations pertaining to significant or material related party transactions in the past three years?	**OECD Principle III:** (B) Insider trading and abusive dealing should be prohibited **ICGN 2.11.1 Related party transactions** Companies should have a process for reviewing and monitoring any related party transaction. A committee of independent directors should review significant related party transactions to determine whether they are in the best interests of the company and if so to determine what terms are fair. **ICGN 2.11.2 Director conflicts of interest** Companies should have a process for identifying and managing any conflicts of interest directors may have. If a director has an interest in a matter under consideration by the board, then the director should not participate in those discussions and the board should follow any further appropriate processes. Individual directors should be conscious of shareholder and public perceptions and seek to avoid situations where there might be an appearance of a conflict of interest. **ICGN 8.5 Shareholder rights of action** Shareholders should be afforded rights of action and remedies which are readily accessible in order to redress conduct of company which treats them inequitably. Minority shareholders should be afforded protection and remedies against abusive or oppressive conduct.

C.   Role of stakeholders

C.1	The rights of stakeholders that are established by law or through mutual agreements are to be respected.	Guiding Reference
C.1.1(P)	Have there been any violations of any laws pertaining to labour/employment/consumer/insolvency/commercial/competition or environmental issues?	**OECD Principle IV:** (A) The rights of stakeholders that are established by law or through mutual agreements are to be respected.

C.2	Where stakeholders participate in the corporate governance process, they should have access to relevant, sufficient and reliable information on a timely and regular basis.	Guiding Reference
C.2.1(P)	Has the company faced any sanctions by regulators for failure to make announcements within the requisite time period for material events?	**OECD Principle IV:** (B) Where stakeholders participate in the corporate governance process, they should have access to relevant, sufficient and reliable information on a timely and regular basis.

D.   Disclosure and Transparency

D.1	Sanctions from regulator on financial reports	Guiding Reference
D.1.1(P)	Did the company receive a "qualified opinion" in its external audit report?	**OECD Principle V: Disclosure and Transparency** (B) Information should be prepared and disclosed in accordance with high quality standards of accounting and financial and non-financial disclosures. (C) An annual audit should be conducted by an independent, competent and qualified, auditor in order to provide an external and objective assurance to the board and shareholders that the financial statements fairly represent the financial position and performance of the company in all material respects.
D.1.2(P)	Did the company receive an "adverse opinion" in its external audit report?	
D.1.3(P)	Did the company receive a "disclaimer opinion" in its external audit report?	(D) External auditors should be accountable to the shareholders and owe a duty to the company to exercise due professional care in the conduct of the audit. **ICGN 6.2 Annual audit** The annual audit carried out on behalf of shareholders is an essential part of the checks and balances required at a company. It should provide an independent and objective opinion that the financial statements fairly represent the financial position and performance of the company in all material respects, give a true and fair view of the affairs of the company and are in compliance with applicable laws and regulations.
D.1.4(P)	Has the company in the past year revised its financial statements for reasons other than changes in accounting policies?	**ICGN 7.3 Affirmation of financial statements** The board of directors and the appropriate officers of the company should affirm at least annually the accuracy of the company's financial statements or financial accounts.

D.1	Sanctions from regulator on financial reports	Guiding Reference
		International Auditing Standard (ISA) No. 705 "Modifications to the Opinion in the Independent Auditor's Report" (2009). Paras. 7, 8 and 9 specify the three types of modifications to the auditor's opinion; that is, Qualified opinion, Adverse opinion, and Disclaimer opinion respectively.

E.   Responsibilities of the Board

E.1	Compliance with listing rules, regulations and applicable laws	Guiding Reference
E.1.1(P)	Is there any evidence that the company has not complied with any listing rules and regulations over the past year apart from disclosure rules?	**OECD Principle VI (D):** (7) Ensuring the integrity of the corporation's accounting and financial reporting systems, including the independent audit, and that appropriate systems of control are in place, in particular, systems for risk management, financial and operational control, and compliance with the law and relevant standards. Companies are also well advised to set up internal programmes and procedures to promote compliance with applicable laws, regulations and standards, including statutes to criminalise bribery of foreign officials that are required to be enacted by the OECD Anti-bribery Convention and measures designed to control other forms of bribery and corruption. Moreover, compliance must also relate to other laws and regulations such as those covering securities, competition and work and safety conditions. Such compliance programmes will also underpin the company's ethical code.
E.1.2(P)	Have there been any instances where non-executive directors/commissioner have resigned and raised any issues of governance-related concerns?	**UK CODE (JUNE 2010)** A.4.3 Where directors have concerns which cannot be resolved about the running of the company or a proposed action, they should ensure that their concerns are recorded in the board minutes. On resignation, a non-executive director should provide a written statement to the chairman, for circulation to the board, if they have any such concerns.

E.2	Board Appraisal	Guiding Reference
E.2.1(P)	Does the Company have any independent directors/commissioners who have served for more than nine years or two terms (whichever is higher) in the same capacity?	**OECD Principle V:** (C) An annual audit should be conducted by an independent, competent and qualified, auditor in order to provide an external and objective assurance to the board and shareholders that the financial statements fairly represent the financial position and performance of the company in all material respects. Examples of other provisions to underpin auditor independence include, a total ban or severe limitation on the nature of non-audit work which can be undertaken by an auditor for their audit client, mandatory rotation of auditors (either partners or in some cases the audit partnership), a temporary ban on the employment of an ex-auditor by the audited company and prohibiting auditors or their dependents from having a financial stake or management role in the companies they audit.
E.2.2(P)	Did the company fail to identify who are the independent director(s)/commissioner(s)?	**ICGN 2.4 Composition and structure of the board** **ICGN 2.4.1 Skills and experience** **ICGN 2.4.3 Independence**
E.2.3(P)	Does the company have any independent directors/non- executive/commissioners who serve on a total of more than five boards of publicly-listed companies?	**OECD Principle VI (E):** (3) Board members should be able to commit themselves effectively to their responsibilities. Service on too many boards can interfere with the performance of board members. Companies may wish to consider whether multiple board memberships by the same person are compatible with effective board performance and disclose the information to shareholders.

E.3	External Audit	Guiding Reference
E.3.1(P)	Are any of the directors or senior management a former employee or partner of the current external auditor (in the past 2 years)?	**OECD Principle V:** (C) An annual audit should be conducted by an independent, competent and qualified, auditor in order to provide an external and objective assurance to the board and shareholders that the financial statements fairly represent the financial position and performance of the company in all material respects.

E.3	External Audit	Guiding Reference
		Examples of other provisions to underpin auditor independence include, a total ban or severe limitation on the nature of non-audit work which can be undertaken by an auditor for their audit client, mandatory rotation of auditors (either partners or in some cases the audit partnership), a temporary ban on the employment of an ex-auditor by the audited company and prohibiting auditors or their dependents from having a financial stake or management role in the companies they audit.

E.4	Board structure and composition	Guiding Reference
E.4.1(P)	Has the chairman been the company CEO in the last three years?	

Annex 2: ACGS Scoring Guide

There are two levels to the ACGS

Level 1: Five Major Sections that correspond to OECD Principles	No. of Items	Weight
Part A. Rights of Shareholders	25	10
Part B. Equitable Treatment of Shareholders	18	15
Part C. Role of Stakeholders	21	10
Part D. Disclosure and Transparency	41	25
Part E. Board Responsibility	74	40
Level 1 Total	**179**	**100**
Level 2: Two Additional Sections		
Bonus (practices beyond minimum standards)	11	Maximum Points
Penalty (for poor practices)	22	26 points
Level 2 Total	**33**	**-59 points**
TOTAL	**212**	**126**